Tips on Taping

Language Recording in the Social Sciences

Wayne B. Dickerson
Lonna J. Dickerson

William Carey Library

533 HERMOSA STREET • SOUTH PASADENA, CALIF. 91030

In accord with some of the most recent thinking in the aca-
demic press, the William Carey Library is pleased to present
this scholarly book which has been prepared from an author-
edited and author-prepared camera-ready manuscript.

Library of Congress Cataloging in Publication Data

Dickerson, Wayne B   1942-
    Tips on taping.

    Bibliography: p.
    Includes index.
    1. Language and languages--Study and teaching--
Audio-visual aids. 2. Phonotapes in education.
I. Dickerson, Lonna J., 1942-   joint author.
II. Title.
P53.D45   621.389'3   76-50023
ISBN 0-87808-147-X

Published by the William Carey Library
533 Hermosa Street
South Pasadena, Calif. 91030
Telephone 213-682-2047

PRINTED IN THE UNITED STATES OF AMERICA

Contents

PART ONE

SELECTION AND CARE OF RECORDING EQUIPMENT

iii

PART TWO

OPERATION OF RECORDING EQUIPMENT

Figures

Preface

Tape recorders have been used for language work from the time
they became available to the public in the 1930's. Certain
characteristics of recorders and tape are especially appropriate
for this purpose. They permit material to be gathered at any
time, in any place, programmed in any way for any purpose, and
stored for any length of time. It is no wonder that individuals
who have a professional concern with spoken language material
have found the tape recorder an extremely valuable, if not indispensable, tool.

Unfortunately, the serious language recordist has never been
well served by the recording industry nor by popular books, pam-
phlets, and articles on recording. Equipment and publications
have been aimed at a general audience whose interest in tape recorders is primarily for entertainment--for having fun or for
playing music. The serious language recordist who asks for help
with his particular problems is met consistently with the common
but simplistic view that he needs nothing special for his task--
no special equipment, no special quality, no special techniques
or skills. While this may be true for the language recordist in
the general audience, it certainly is not true for the group we
address.

Language recordists in our audience deal with language in a
serious way, if not professionally. They represent many different disciplines and interests. There are the linguists and
phonoticians who have always focused on linguistic detail and
often subject their data to acoustic analysis. In our audience
are dialectologists and sociolinguists who look at regional and
social correlates of speech differences. The latter group, in

particular, has strong scholarly interests in recording natural, casual speech. We have much to say to the field anthropologist, the anthropological linguist, and the folklorist as they investigate on-location speech events of various kinds. Also addressed are psycholinguists, speech therapists, and educational psychologists, all of whom have interests in child language development. For these individuals, the tape recorder is more than a convenience. Expertise in its use clearly facilitates their research and in some cases makes the kind of research they do possible.

Language laboratory directors are prominent in our audience. They must evaluate and select many kinds of equipment and supplies. Furthermore, they are responsible to train their lab personnel in the function, use, and care of equipment--how recorders work, how to bulk erase, copy, repair, and store tapes, how to do preventative maintenance on all equipment.

Another important group of recordists are language teachers. For them, the tape recorder is a basic tool in their audio-visual repertoire. Because of their knowledge of drill techniques, language teachers are the ones most frequently asked to make or upgrade tape recordings for classroom, language lab, and now for the audio component of computer-assisted instruction. Good ideas, however, do not make good tapes; also required are appropriate recording and editing techniques. To equip these individuals, numerous authorities on language teaching have called for tape recording seminars to be part of every teacher training program.

Language learners are also addressed: students studying foreign languages, missionary language learners, members of diplomatic or advisory missions overseas, and many, many others. They know that language learning research and practical experience have shown the tape recorder to be of great value in language study. To realize this value, however, it takes a knowledgeable approach to recording.

There are numerous other language recordists we might mention. In fact, anyone who does face-to-face interviewing is potentially a language recordist--for instance, reporters and historians of various kinds who are interested in oral history--history in the making or history already made. The list goes on: Bible translators, ethnomusicologists, simultaneous translators, and still others.

Despite the diversity of their interests in language material, these recordists hold in common the need to make intelligent equipment choices, the need to use their equipment to fullest advantage, and the need to get top quality performance

from their equipment year after year. *Tips on Taping* is intended
to provide help tailored to the particular needs of language recordists. The fact is, the right equipment for every language
recording task is available on the market somewhere. Special
techniques which are best suited to those tasks are also known.
But for any particular recordist, what is right? What is best?
Different circumstances require different equipment and recording
techniques. In this book, we can help you find the answer to
these questions. Furthermore, the answer will be nontechnical
and straightforward.

As a nontechnical, practical guide, this book is not for the
audio specialist. He has the technical background and instruments to test and evaluate recording equipment; he has professional recorders, mikes, and mixers; he has sound-proof studios
for his use. For him, there are numerous technical treatments
on the fine points of recording.

Tips on Taping is for those who are specialists in fields
other than recorder technology. Most in our audience must use
semiprofessional or nonprofessional equipment of various sorts
and use it in less than optimal circumstances. They must nevertheless come up with superb recordings for their various purposes
which may be research, teaching, or learning. The message of
this book is that you do not have to be an audio expert in order
to make expert-sounding tapes. The know-how is in the following
pages.

Throughout this book, we assume no background knowledge of
audio equipment on the part of the recordist. However, some in
our audience are quite familiar with recorders, their use, and
their care. To accommodate different levels of sophistication
about recording, we recommend the following. If the reader is
interested in only pithy advice for bothersome choices he must
make, he may be satisfied with index references and the TIPS
which are set off throughout the text and contain just such information. On the other hand, if the reader wants to find out
more about a topic, the supporting text will fill that need.
For the person who is interested in even more detail, we provide
notes, appendices, and a useful bibliography.

Part One is devoted to the selection and care of recording
equipment. This is an especially good time to deal with these
matters because the recording industry is just now settling on
the basic formats which will be with us for the foreseeable
future: two- and four-track cassette recorders, eight-track
cartridge recorders, two-, four-, and eight-track open-reel
machines all of which record and play back. Much of the ambi-
guity and uncertainty connected with competing formats is now
gone; the choices are more clearcut.

In this part, the language recordist will find answers to questions like the following. Which recorder format and degree of quality is best for the kind of language work that I am doing? What kind of microphone is best suited to my circumstances? What kind of tape will not deteriorate in the hot or humid, cold or dry climatic extremes in which I will be working? What do I need in order to cope with a foreign power supply?

Equipment evaluation and care need not be expensive to be good. We have supplied information on easy ways to tropicalize equipment, to check speed accuracy and monitor it over time, to evaluate tape construction and quality, and so on.

In Part Two, we deal with questions about using equipment to record and to edit. We present the ideal recording situation but also show how to cope with less than the ideal. In this way, we provide guidance not only for the recordist whose equipment and tape never leave the temperature and humidity controlled environment of laboratory or studio, but also for the recordist who has to "rough it" on-location where acoustic conditions are poor and equipment demands extra care.

In this part, the recordist can find answers to questions such as: How can I be sure of getting the right record level every time I record? What is the easiest way to record an interview, record at a distance from the subject, record when I cannot personally be present? What are some simple but effective editing techniques for making my recordings sound professional?

In sum, for the recordist whose product must bear the mark of care, *Tips on Taping* can put recording technology at his command.

. . . .

A special word of thanks is due to James R. Payne, III, an audio engineer at the University of Illinois, for his critical reading of this book for technical accuracy, and for his helpful suggestions throughout. Any inaccuracies which remain are, of course, the sole responsibility of the authors.

Part One

Selection and Care of Recording Equipment

Introduction to Part One

Recording equipment is composed of three basic elements: the recorder, the microphone, and the tape. In this part, we are concerned with how to select the proper equipment and how to give it the care it requires.

A central question of those engaged in language work is, What kind of recording tools do I need for the job I have to do? In this part of the book, we try to deal with this question in a serious and helpful way. The approach we use is to ask you to consider exactly what your job is and in what circumstances you will be doing it. Your situation and the kinds of uses you intend for your equipment should guide you to the tools you need. For this reason, all of our discussions on selecting equipment are use oriented.

But selection cannot be separated from care of equipment; they go together like hand and glove. The selection of equipment at the same time presents a care problem. If you choose a recorder, mike, or reel of tape for its particular characteristics and quality, it is very likely you are interested that the characteristics and quality you have purchased remain intact: thus, a care problem. Interestingly enough, the careful selection of equipment is also the best preparation for proper care. In the course of selecting a piece of equipment, you should investigate it thoroughly and become intimately familiar with how it works and why. It is such knowledge of your equipment, whether recorder, mike, or tape, that is essential background to top quality care.

1 Tape Recorder Selection

It was not long ago that the term *tape recorder* brought to mind only one picture--one general shape, size, and function. Recorder manufacturers were few, and the infant industry supplied a small demand. Recently, however, the image of a tape recorder has become very fuzzy indeed. A myriad shapes, sizes, and variations on the basic recording theme have appeared on the market. With hundreds of manufacturers producing recording equipment, the industry is booming.

These dramatic changes have had a marked effect on the consumer. Once there were few instruments to choose from; the choice of a tape recorder was relatively simple, even enjoyable. Now, recorder shopping, if taken seriously, has become an awesome job. The array of choices is phenomenal and, for many buyers, the task of selecting only one recorder from among the choices has been filled with uncertainty, frustration, even exasperation.

This situation has forced a change in the approach to recorder buying. If he hopes to avoid a costly mistake, today's prospective purchaser must do some homework before entering the equipment maze. Only through investigation can the buyer find enough information on which to base an intelligent and satisfying decision about equipment.

There are five essential questions which every recorder shopper must answer before purchasing a machine.

1. What *category* of recorder do I want?

2. What *current* should power the recorder?

3. What recording *quality* do I need?

4. How many *tracks* should I get?

5. How *easy to use* and how *durable* is the recorder?

Answers to these questions will differ widely according to
your individual circumstances and needs. It is through such
answers, however, that you can arrive at a description of the
recorder you need. To help you answer some of these questions,
we will try to relate them to practical situations. We will
offer suggestions and guidelines in the form of periodic TIPS
throughout the text, bearing in mind your interest in recording
language data.

WHAT CATEGORY OF RECORDER DO I WANT?

The range of recorder categories is wide. There is no need
to discuss the whole range in detail, however, since only a
segment of it is applicable for most language recording purposes. We will consider the range briefly only to narrow it to
that applicable segment. The easiest way to treat the variety
of recorder categories is through a discussion of four pairs of
terms, as shown in Figure 1.

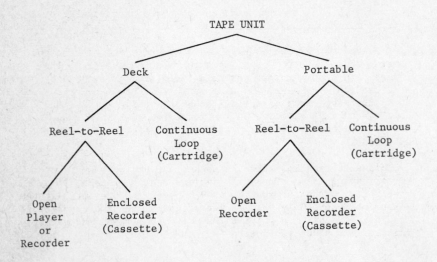

Fig. 1. Diagram of Recorder Formats

Deck versus Portable

Deck machines are bare-boned instruments without power amplifiers or speakers. They are intended to be one of a number
of components in a larger system which may include a hi-fi
turntable, FM tuner, stereo amplifiers and speakers. Decks are
not considered portable because they are not self-contained
units.

Portable machines come complete with amplifiers and speakers.
While some instruments are so heavy that their portability is
doubtful, they are nonetheless portable in the sense of being
self-contained.

The language recordist will ordinarily choose the portable
machine, not only because it can be taken where needed, but
also because of its modest cost when compared with decks and
ancillary equipment. Decks, however, should not be dismissed
lightly. It is quite generally the case that a look at decks
today will predict the features and quality to be found on
portables tomorrow.

Player versus Recorder

Players are, as the name implies, machines which are designed with a playback function only. They cannot record, but
play prerecorded tapes. While there are some reel-to-reel
player decks, many cartridge machines are exclusively players.
Without the record capability, it is impossible to meet any
language recording needs. Thus, the most serviceable category
of the two is the machine which both plays and records.

Reel-to-Reel versus Continuous Loop (Cartridge)

The terms reel-to-reel and continuous loop refer to the number and kind of reels used on particular machines. The terms
also serve to distinguish two large categories of machines.
One category, reel-to-reel, uses two reels. During operation,
the tape on one reel (known as the feed or supply reel) passes
through the recorder to fill the second reel (known as the
take-up reel). The second category of machines uses only one
reel. The tape on the reel is pieced together at the ends to
form a complete endless loop. A special kind of reel is used
which allows the tape to be pulled from the inside hub of the
reel while at the same time winding the tape back onto the
reel's outside circumference.

Machines using the single-reel arrangement are called cartridge machines. For those concerned with language recording,
the cartridge machine, while fascinating, offers some serious

disadvantages. First, cartridge recorders generally have no
fast forward or rewind speed. If a faster forward speed is
available, it must operate considerably slower than a true fast
forward. Thus, there is no quick way to bypass material on the
tape. Secondly, there is typically no index counter to help
find a particular place on the tape. Third, since reverse tape
movement is not possible either, immediate replay of program
content cannot be done. To listen again to any one portion of
tape, you must wait until that portion comes around again.
Fourth, material must be carefully timed to fit the length of
tape available on one track. Typically, the maximum length of
one track is twenty minutes (eighty minutes on four tracks)
which does not offer sufficient uninterrupted recording time for
many purposes. If the material has not been well timed to fit
into twenty-minute segments, the recording will be spread between two tracks. When the machine changes tracks while recording, there will be a slight loss of material and an audible
click preserved on the tape. Fifth, the tape loop does wear
out. The lubricant on the tape breaks down because of the tape
constantly rubbing on itself. This will show up as variations
in speed accuracy.

   None of the above drawbacks are particularly important when
listening to prerecorded tapes, but when the need to record
arises, all of these points are important. Reel-to-reel machines, on the other hand, suffer none of these problems. They
move in true fast forward and reverse, have index counters, are
unencumbered by matters of wearability or tape length where
literally hours of uninterrupted recording time are available.
Therefore, the decision for the language recordist is not a
difficult one to make.

Open versus Enclosed

   The distinction between open and enclosed refers to the
housing of the tape and separates two broad recorder categories.
The enclosed reel-to-reel accurately describes the cassette magazine: two small reels (less than two inches in diameter) enclosed in a plastic case. The tape on these reels is about
1/8-inch wide. Open reel-to-reel operation involves two reels
which are not enclosed. The tape used on these reels is 1/4-
inch wide.

   Both open-reel and cassette recorders offer possibilities for
the language recordist. The two recorders present many parallel
capabilities: playback and record, fast forward and reverse,
two track and four track, monophonic and stereophonic recording,
AC and AC/DC operation, and so forth.

Some considerations--nonparallel aspects--may be significant in the final decision about recorder category. Happily, the major differences between open- and enclosed-reel recorders are no longer necessarily differences in recording quality. The differences are largely matters of physical characteristics which make each recorder type particularly appropriate for specific applications. The principal distinguishing characteristics are mentioned here briefly. A fuller discussion is provided later in this chapter.

Cassette machines are the smallest, most lightweight, recorders on the market. From the point of view of portability and inconspicuous use, they must rank first. For convenience of operation, cassettes also score high because the magazines are easy to use and tape threading and spilling are eliminated by the enclosed reels. With knock-out tabs on the magazines to prevent accidental erasure, these recorders are considered virtually foolproof. For track compatibility from recorder to recorder, cassettes are unrivaled: Almost all recordings, regardless of track format, are usable on all machines. These and other design specifications are standardized. Finally, but not least in importance, cassette recorders are the least expensive machines available.

On the other side of the scale, open-reel recorders are unmatched in *continuous* recording time because of having a larger tape capacity than cassettes. Editing by splicing, very difficult with cassette tape, is easily done with open-reel tape. Special features such as sound-on-sound and record monitoring (through earphone or headset) are almost exclusively the domain of open-reel recorders.

Just how important these various characteristics are to the recordist depends entirely on his projected recording applications. For this reason, a clear statement of intended uses of the recorder is an indispensable prerequisite to the choice of recorder category. In many cases, the ideal will be to have a representative of each category in order to gain the advantages each brings to the task of recording language in diverse situations. As will become apparent, the value of the cassette and open-reel recorder combination is far greater than the value of the units separately.

TIP: We have followed the diagram in Figure 1 in order to narrow the recorder categories to those most likely to serve the needs of the language recordist. We have suggested two categories, the *open* and *enclosed reel-to-reel portable recorders*. The choice between open-reel and cassette revolves around the specific configuration of recording needs. The combination of the two recorder types will cover the full range of language recording demands and will add versatility besides.

WHAT CURRENT SHOULD POWER THE RECORDER?

Tape recorders can be divided into three power categories: (1) AC-only, (2) AC/DC, and (3) battery-only (DC). For open-reel recorders, the choice should be restricted to AC-only or AC/DC, because battery-only recorders are almost universally of very poor quality. Cassette machines may have any of the three types of power requirements. The choice of a DC-only cassette recorder, however, is generally not a practical choice; re-corders have voracious appetites for electrical power. There-fore, to avoid the continual purchase of batteries and to secure the option to use available AC to conserve battery power, we recommend that a battery-operated cassette also have some pro-vision for using AC. The AC adapters of many recorders are built in; others are external depending on the size of the re-corder itself. In the following discussion, we will focus on machines with AC-only or AC/DC power requirements.

What are the crucial factors which will determine whether an AC or an AC/DC machine should be chosen? There are five con-siderations which will affect your decision.

Local Power Supply

For residents of the United States, Canada, and other areas using 110-120 volts, 60-cycle current, any concern over a difficult-to-use power supply may be almost irrelevant. But for those planning to use a tape recorder where the available power is different, the question of local power supply is par-ticularly pertinent. The following guidelines may be helpful.

If alternating current (AC) is available, whether 110-120 volts or 220-240 volts, an AC recorder may be used, provided that the current is relatively free from fluctuation and that appropriate cycle conversion equipment is used where necessary. For a discussion of conversion equipment, see Appendix 1.

An AC/DC recorder is better (1) if the current fluctuates wildly, (2) if there is direct current, or (3) if no current is available other than what is present in common flashlight bat-teries. For poor-power or no-power situations, battery opera-tion is essential. The optional AC provision of the recorder permits the recordist to take advantage of AC power whenever it is available in order to conserve battery life.

If an AC/DC recorder seems to be a possibility for you, a supply of DC power must be assured before you can use the machine away from AC mains. Some consideration should be given to how the needed DC supply can be obtained.

Standard size dry cells can be purchased almost world-wide. But buying batteries overseas can be expensive as well as risky. In many places, batteries cost much more than at home. What is worse, it is impossible to tell by sight a fully charged battery from a dead one. If no other choice is available for DC power, the best preparation is to purchase a small (pocket size) battery tester.[1] With this inexpensive instrument, you can check the battery charge before purchase.

The life of some batteries can be extended by using a recharging unit adaptable to AC mains. Although charging the common carbon-zinc cell is impractical as well as hazardous, the rechargeable-type alkaline battery can be successfully rejuvenated provided it is not permitted to become exhausted. The best rechargeable battery available, however, is the nickel-cadmium (ni-cad) battery, which can be recharged almost indefinitely. Appendix 1 provides a discussion and evaluation of carbon-zinc, alkaline, and nickel-cadmium cells.

An increasing number of AC/DC recorders come equipped with a built-in recharging circuit. Rechargeable batteries are rejuvenated in the machine by using the AC adapter to plug the recorder into an AC supply for a period of time. During that time, recording and playback functions of most machines can still be used. If the recharger is not built in, external recharging units are widely available.

The advantage of the rechargeable battery is obvious and the cost well worth the investment. However, only the local power situation can determine whether or not this option should be considered. If AC is accessible for sufficiently long periods of time, such as six to eight hours per day, rechargeable batteries can be maintained. If not, this answer to DC power will be of little use.

Use of Recorder away from AC Power Supply

Although steady, usable AC may be at hand for an AC-only recorder, one's recording needs may require that recording be done away from the AC supply. In this case, an AC/DC recorder is the answer.

Manufacturers of many AC/DC machines make an adapter for using the tape recorder from a car battery via the cigarette lighter socket. If your recording or playback needs can be met during travel or while you are close to your vehicle, this accessory can be a real asset.

Watts Output (Volume or Audio Power)

How large an audience must be able to hear the recording? If the recorder will be used only for individual or small group listening, an AC/DC machine is adequate. These recorders have much smaller outputs than AC machines. While some AC/DC machines can boast of two watts of audio power, most fall within the range of .50 to 1 watt. Unless hooked into an auxiliary amplifying system, however, this volume will not be sufficient for larger audiences. Only AC machines can provide the necessary volume for large groups.

> TIP: AC/DC machines are adequate for individual or small group work. For large rooms, look for an AC recorder with at least five to ten watts output.

Some recorders can double as public address systems capable of amplifying the speaker's voice as he talks into the microphone. If this is an important feature to you, consider the size of your audience to determine the power output needed.

Maximum Reel Size

How large a reel of tape can you anticipate using on the machine? For cassette recorders, only one size is available; for open-reel recorders there are several sizes. Open reels come in three common sizes, 7-inch, 5-inch, and 3-inch diameters, although other sizes are also available. Most AC-only recorders can accommodate 7-inch reels of tape. This capacity permits the use of all smaller reels on the recorder as well. AC/DC machines ordinarily take a maximum of a 3-inch or a 5-inch reel, but a few also provide for a 7-inch reel.

Because of the need to play prerecorded 7-inch tapes, a 7-inch reel capacity may be important to you. Although more playing time is provided by this larger reel size, a 5-inch reel capacity is large enough for the needs of most persons. There are at least three factors to recommend the 5-inch reel.

First, thin tape (1 mil, 1/2 mil) allows much more tape to be put on a reel than is possible with 1 1/2-mil tape. For example, when using a two-track recorder at a speed of 1 7/8 inches per second (ips), a 5-inch reel of 1 1/2-mil tape will permit about two hours of recording. By contrast, 1 mil gives more than three hours, and 1/2 mil offers a maximum of about six and a half hours on one reel.

Second, slower tape speeds (3 3/4, 1 7/8, and 15/16 ips, rather than 7 1/2 ips) can increase the recording time per reel of tape by two, four, or eight times depending on the speed

used. As an illustration, using 1-mil tape on a two-track recorder at 7 1/2 ips, the tape will play for forty-eight minutes.
The slower speeds will stretch the same tape much longer: at
3 3/4 ips, about one and a half hours; at 1 7/8 ips, more than
three hours; and at 15/16 ips, about six and a half hours are
possible.

Finally, by using a four-track instead of a two-track recorder, twice as much recording can be put on a length of tape.
Therefore, the illustrations given above can be multiplied by
two as an example of the amount of time added to the same reel
of tape. Or, by using 1/2-mil tape at 15/16 ips, a 5-inch reel
of tape will last twenty-five and a half hours.

Any one or any combination of these three factors will make
5-inch reels amply satisfactory for the majority of language recording uses. For quick reference to recording time for reels
of different sizes, backings of different thicknesses, and tapes
of different lengths, see Appendix 2.

Recorders capable of accommodating only very small reels (3
inch, 3 1/4 inch), may be adequate for some purposes. The
amount of tape contained on a 3-inch reel, however, is often not
sufficient for most practical purposes without constant turning
of reels. The tendency will be to go to very thin tape in order
to increase recording time. But thin tape and small reel capacity is a dangerous combination. The smaller the reel hub,
the greater the stress on the tape between the reels. While a
5-inch reel, when almost empty, will increase the stress
slightly above that present between two 7-inch reels, a 3-inch
reel doubles the stress. Thus thin tape on a 3-inch reel or
smaller is very likely to be stretched and distorted. At the
opposite extreme, some language laboratories and other recording facilities use take-up reels with extra-large hubs to minimize stress even more, and some professional recorders have
tension switches to compensate for stress differences.

TIP: The choice between an AC-only or AC/DC machine may
depend on the size of reel that must be used. If this is
not an issue, a 7-inch reel capacity is best for AC-only
machines. For AC/DC recorders, a 5-inch reel capacity is
recommended. For cassettes, there is only one standard
size magazine, limiting the amount of time to 30, 60, 90,
120, or 180 minutes (for two-track mono or four-track
stereo) depending on the amount of tape in the magazine.

Weight and Size of Machine

Will it be necessary to carry the recorder for long periods
of time? If so, weight may warrant consideration. What is

light for one person may be heavy for another, but, in general, machines weighing up to ten to twelve pounds can be handled comfortably for short distances. The recordist's demand for a high degree of portability will encourage him to select AC/DC powered recorders. If the machine will be moved only periodically, being used primarily in one place, weight may not figure importantly in your decision. While either an AC-only or an AC/DC machine would serve equally well, the AC-only machine would be preferred where AC is available. This preference will become clear when we turn to a discussion of motors, wow and flutter.

Weight is one consideration in the choice of recorder power requirements; size is another. If recording applications demand concealed or inconspicuous equipment, physical dimensions may need to be as small as possible. Immediately precluded are AC-only recorders, the largest and heaviest of portables. Most AC/DC open-reel recorders may also be too large. At their smallest they are comparable to a desk dictionary; at their largest they are the size of an ordinary briefcase. In weight they range generally from seven to seventeen pounds with the majority between nine and twelve pounds.

Cassette portables come in three sizes: standard, pocket, and miniature. Standard cassette machines are roughly the size of a desk dictionary, weighing three to twelve pounds, with most clustering between four and seven pounds. These, like their open-reel counterparts, may still be too large. The best answer to the small recorder requirement is the pocket cassette. This cassette recorder will in fact fit in a coat pocket, being roughly the size of a pocket paperback book. Weight is pocket-size, too: 1 1/2 to 2 1/2 pounds. Standard cassette magazines are used, so that as much recording time is available when using a pocket cassette recorder as when using a standard cassette recorder.

Miniature cassette recorders are the size of a pack of cigarettes and weigh between six ounces and one pound. As attractive as these measurements sound, miniature cassette recorders are not recommended in general for several reasons. The principal reason is that the tape is almost universally rim-driven and not capstan-driven, yielding widely varying record and playback speeds. The cassette magazines are also miniature but are not generally available. Most problematic, however, is that there is very little recording time per cassette cartridge. The need to flip or change magazines frequently is not ordinarily a desirable feature for equipment that is to remain out of sight, unnoticed or untended for more than fifteen minutes. Finally, recording quality has not yet progressed beyond what is sufficient for dictation purposes.

TIP: The need for lightweight portability selects AC/DC over AC-only recorders. The need for very small size selects pocket AC/DC cassette recorders over standard cassette and open-reel recorders. Avoid miniature cassette recorders, except for highly specialized purposes in which their major defects will not be crucial.

To summarize, the five variables discussed above have pointed to the most relevant factors involved in selecting recorder power. In the following section, we will consider recorder quality.

WHAT RECORDING QUALITY DO I NEED?

Quality begins with the transport system, the mechanical components of the recorder which move the tape across the recording head. If the movement is uneven or jerky, no matter how fine the electrical system may be, good quality cannot be realized. It has been accurately observed that it is the mechanical characteristics of the recorder which separate the professional models from the semi-professional and home models. We will first consider the mechanical *transport system*, then turn to the electrical *record/playback system*.

Transport System

The job of the transport system is to move the tape, whether for recording, playback, or for quickly locating sections ahead (fast forward) or past (fast reverse). The system does its job by means of one or more *motors, linked to the tape*, pulling it along at a fixed *speed* with a particular *degree of accuracy*. Differences in quality can be seen in each of these aspects of the transport mechanism. We will point out these differences as we go along.

The Motor. The motor is the workhorse of the recorder. It operates on AC power in an AC-only recorder or on DC power in an AC/DC machine.

To handle the various transport responsibilities, some recorders employ more than one motor. Such recorders approach professional quality. When more than one motor is used in the transport system, fewer mechanical linkages are needed. Because mechanical linkages deteriorate in time, the fewer linkages (belts, pulleys, gears), the fewer problems. Multiple-motor systems, then, are generally more dependable, have fewer breakdowns, and run faster and smoother in fast forward and reverse than single-motor systems.

The vast majority of recorders, including nearly all AC/DC
machines, use only one motor for all functions. There are many
semi-professional instruments in this group of single-motor recorders.

The motor ultimately regulates the movement of the tape
across the record/playback heads of the recorder. If the tape
is to pass the heads at a constant speed, the motor must rotate
at a constant speed. Motors differ in the degree to which speed
accuracy is possible.

There are two main types of AC motors, the induction type
(shaded-pole) and the hysteresis synchronous type. Induction
motors are dependent upon the AC line *voltage* for their speed.
Changes in voltage, such as occur when turning on appliances
which draw heavily on the current (noticeable as a slight dim-
ming or flickering of a light), will cause speed changes. Less
expensive recorders use induction motors. The more expensive
synchronous motors are found on better machines. They maintain
constant speed because the speed is dependent upon power line
frequency (50 or 60 cycles) which remains constant even though
voltage may fluctuate. As compared with DC motors, both types
of AC motors, being heavier and more powerful, are considerably
more resistant to speed variations caused by sticking tape or
pressure pads, warped and dragging reels, or a dirty transport
mechanism.

DC motors tend to vary in speed as the voltage of batteries
drops. In better AC/DC machines, a substantial improvement has
come with the incorporation of servo systems which monitor the
speed of the motor and correct for slight changes. The effect
is a constant motor speed over a wide range of power levels.

TIP: While more than one motor is a mark of good quality,
it is not a mark of poor quality for a recorder to have
only one motor. Unless stated otherwise, assume an induction motor in AC-only models and a non-servo system in
AC/DC recorders. Both hysteresis synchronous motors and
servo systems are desirable, but the servo system is especially important for serious recording when batteries
other than nickel-cadmium are used. See Appendix 1 for a
discussion of battery characteristics.

Drive Mechanism. The motor must be linked to the tape in
order to draw the tape through the machine. The means by which
this operation is accomplished is called the drive mechanism.
There are two common types of drive mechanisms on the market:
capstan-drive and rim-drive. It is important to understand the
characteristics of these two mechanisms in order to evaluate recorder quality.

Good machines, whether open-reel or cassette, will always
have capstans; toy recorders and miniature cassettes may not.
The capstan, a vertical rod linked to the motor, is located on
the take-up reel side of the recording head opposite the rubber
(or pinch) roller. The tape is pinched between the capstan and
the rubber roller. As the rod rotates, it pulls the tape off
the feed reel and past the recorder heads at a constant speed.
The value of the capstan lies in the uniformity with which it
moves the tape.

Borrowing from computer technology, professional recorders
use two capstans, one on either side of the heads. This arrangement is called closed-loop tape drive. It provides the ul-
timate in speed accuracy and in addition improves the frequency
response because of closer tape-head contact.

At the other extreme, some recorders do not have capstans at
all. Rather, the motor is linked to the take-up reel of the
recorder. This type of recorder is known as a rim-drive recorder. The speed of tape movement, then, varies with the diameter of the tape on the take-up reel. At the beginning of the
reel, the diameter is small and the speed of the tape is slow;
at the end, the diameter is large and the speed is therefore
fast. A tape made on a rim-drive recorder should be played back
only on the same recorder, but even then the replay speed may
not be exactly the same as the record speed.

For any serious recording, constant speed is essential, not
only to be able to use a tape on any other capstan-drive machine, but also to assure true reproduction of the sound recorded.

The TIP is self-evident: Be certain the recorder has a
capstan. One will do, and it is easy to spot.

Tape Speed. The motor drives the capstan; the capstan drives
the tape. The crucial question at this point is: At how many
different speeds should the capstan drive the tape? A few comments on tape speeds should help you evaluate this question
critically and answer it correctly for your own needs.

In capstan-drive machines, the tape movement across the recording head is constant and therefore measurable. Tape speed
is conventionally measured in terms of distance per unit of
time. On nonmetric recorders, the distance used is the *inch;* on
metric recorders, the distance is the *centimeter*. For both, the
unit of time is the *second*. Tape speed is therefore in terms of
inches per second (ips) or *centimeters per second* (cm/s). The
most common tape speeds for nonmetric recorders are 7 1/2,
3 3/4, 1 7/8, 15/16 ips. Faster speeds, 30 ips and 15 ips, are

found only on recorders used for professional purposes. Metric
tape speeds are 19, 9.5, 4.75, 2.375 cm/s. In all cases, each
speed is one half of its neighbor to the left and double its
neighbor to the right as listed. Cassettes run only at the
standard speed of 1 7/8 ips.

We have said that the presence of a speed control is essential and that more than one speed setting is desirable. In
considering how many speeds will suit your needs, you should
consider: (1) the effect of speed on recording quality, and
(2) the effect of speed on tape economy.

Two axioms are important here for open-reel recording. The
first is that recording quality goes up as the tape speed gets
faster. That is, with all other variables held constant, better
reproduction will be achieved at 7 1/2 ips than at 3 3/4 ips.
The second axiom is that less tape is used as the tape speed
gets slower. For example, only one-half as much tape will be
used when recording at 3 3/4 ips as will be used when recording
for the same length of time at 7 1/2 ips.

These two axioms work against each other. When we want
quality, we must sacrifice tape length; when we want economy,
we must sacrifice quality. What is the wise way to handle this
opposition?

The presence of more than one speed on an open-reel recorder
makes this dilemma easier to resolve. The guideline should be
this: Judge what quality you want before you begin to record.
Then set the tape speed accordingly. As an illustration, taking
an average machine with three speeds, 7 1/2 ips, 3 3/4 ips, and
1 7/8 ips, the highest quality will be gained at 7 1/2 ips. Use
this speed for music. For less critically judged music or for
fine phonetic distinctions, including language material, 3 3/4
ips is ordinarily sufficient. The slowest speed, and therefore
the poorest quality, should be reserved for such things as taped
letters and lectures, where high quality is not essential.
Thus, by letting the quality desired govern the selection of
tape speed, tape sacrifice is made only where necessary, and
tape conservation is made where possible.

The recommendation, then, is that you should usually cater to
quality rather than to tape economy. It is helpful to recall
that there are other ways to increase the amount of recording
time on an open reel of tape in addition to using slower speeds:
use of thinner tape and use of more tracks.

From this discussion it might seem that cassettes, which
operate at 1 7/8 ips only, are immediately at a disadvantage for
having a single speed. This was true not long ago before

improvements in recording tape oxides, in head construction, and in electronics came along. It is still true to some extent where these improvements are not employed in inexpensive machines. But with these advancements, it is possible to capture the full range of recording quality. Furthermore, quality can be varied intelligently, not by speed adjustments, but by the tape used: the best (and most expensive) tape oxides for the most exacting requirements, ordinary (moderately priced) tape oxides—but not off-brand tape—for less exacting needs. The general recommendation still holds: Prefer quality to economy, but economize when high quality is not required.

> TIP: For open-reel recorders, two speeds (7 1/2 and 3 3/4 ips, or 3 3/4 and 1 7/8 ips) are better than only one. The decision for a third or fourth speed should be weighed carefully against the cost of the extra speed or speeds, the range of recording quality needed, and the possible savings in tape. For cassette recorders, the choice has already been settled; only one speed, 1 7/8 ips, is available. Wise selection of tape oxides provides the best quality when necessary and the best economy when possible.

Wow and Flutter. On the specification sheet that accompanies a recorder, there should be a category of figures called *wow and flutter*. It is one of the few specifications directly related to the cost of the machine. Wow and flutter refers to the sound distortion caused by a lack of uniform tape speed across the recorder heads. It is measured in terms of the percentage of distortion present during record and playback when compared with the undistorted original sound. Wow and flutter is perceived as an unevenness in pitch and volume noticeable especially when playing back sustained musical notes such as in piano music. Obviously, the less wow and flutter, the better.

The percentage of wow and flutter is an index to the quality of the transport system as a whole and is therefore an indication of how truly sound can be recorded and played back without distortion. Indexed is the combined contribution of motors, capstans, and controls. To avoid deterioration of mechanical apparatus over time and to guarantee sustained high quality performance, many professional recorders will use (1) two or three hysteresis synchronous motors which reduce the number of rubber wheels, gears, and belts; (2) two capstans with large flywheels for closed loop drive; (3) solenoid controls for all functions thereby eliminating spring tensions and extra mechanical parts.

These features, however, are not essential for very good wow and flutter ratings on nonprofessional equipment. In general, the smaller the machine, the greater the wow and flutter. For this reason AC/DC machines in particular will perform better

with servo-controlled motors. With use, all machines even under
the best conditions will increase in wow and flutter. Proper
maintenance, as discussed in Chapter 2, will minimize this problem. An important observation is that wow is least at higher
speeds, greatest at lower speeds. Thus, when only one wow and
flutter percentage is given in the specifications, the figure
represents the degree of distortion at the fastest speed.

TIP: Among nonprofessional machines, if the specifications
rate a new recorder as having ±.15 percent or less wow and
flutter, it is very good; ±.15 to .20 percent is good; ±.20
to .25 percent is average. If there is no mention of wow
and flutter for an open-reel or AC cassette recorder, regard
it as suspect. Better AC/DC cassettes, both standard and
pocket, will list wow and flutter, but because small size
and slow speeds work against constant speed, others may not.
Be wary of the latter.

Other Transport System Features. Part of the job of recorder
selection is knowing the difference between *must* and *maybe* features, between the essential and the nonessential. This knowledge is valuable in order to avoid being needlessly oversold.
In the previous sections we have pointed to the essentials; in
this section we draw attention to a mixture of essential and
nonessential transport system features.

1. Tape Lifters. In a later section, we will discuss the
damage that tape can do to the recording head simply through
contact. Ideally, the tape should touch the heads only during
recording or playback. Some provision should be made, therefore, to move the tape away from the heads during fast forward
and fast reverse. Although tape lifters are one of the most
common ways to keep the tape away from the heads, some manufacturers use other devices to achieve the same results. It is
easy for you, the prospective buyer, to tell when there are no
tape lifters or tape-lifter substitutes. In fast forward, you
can see the tape ride on the heads. Also, some recorders may
emit a shrill screech as the magnetic signals on the tape register with the head.

TIP: Be sure the recorder you choose has some means to
separate the tape from the heads during fast forward and
reverse.

2. Automatic Shutoff. Some recorders have a built-in sensing device to stop the recorder when the tape either runs out
or breaks. This is a convenient feature on machines which may
be left unattended for a period of time, such as recorders in a
language laboratory. Although this is an inexpensive feature
found on more and more recorders, it probably should not carry
much weight in your decision about an open-reel recorder.

When considering cassette recorders, the evaluation of automatic shutoff must be different. When a cassette machine empties a reel, the motor continues to pull at the leader which is fixed to the reel hub until the recorder is stopped. To avoid this needless wear, preserve battery life, and reduce the possibility of pulling the leader loose from the hub, the automatic shutoff is more than a convenience for cassette recorders.

3. Automatic Reverse. A few machines, both open-reel and cassette, incorporate a feature which will automatically reverse the direction of tape movement when the feed reel has been emptied or when a sensing device signals. By means of the sensing device, the reels reverse direction and continue playing without being turned over. Although some tape handling is avoided, this convenience must be weighed against the rather high cost of the extra heads used in most models and the expense of a more complex mechanical operation. Because significant expense is required with no improvement (and often loss) in recording and playback quality, it seems unwise to consider this feature to be an important selling point for the language recordist.

To summarize, the task of evaluating the transport system is done partly by visually inspecting the machine for capstan drive, tape lifters, and the desired speed settings and partly by scrutinizing the recorder specifications. In addition, there are several simple tests you can use to check the quality of the transport system. These are mentioned on page 47.

Record/Playback System

It takes two top quality systems to make one top quality tape recording. In the section above, we discussed in some detail the qualities and characteristics of the *transport system*. In this section, we focus on the electrical *record/playback system*.

First, we will take a brief look at the recording and playback process. Then we will examine more closely some of the features of this process that you should understand in order to evaluate this aspect of a recorder.

Because of the complexity of the recording system, most of the tape recorder specifications will be in this section. In order to guide your interpretation of these specifications, we will relate them to recording purposes of various kinds. Since you alone know your needs, some TIPS may help you decide which specifications will satisfy your particular recording demands. A summary of recorder specifications, divided into various quality categories, is given in Figure _, page 32.

Record and Playback Functions. How does a recorder work? Without engaging in a technical explanation, a summary of the basic phases of recording is as follows.

Sound is essentially *vibrating air particles*. The fact that each sound has a different *pattern* of vibrations makes it different from all other sounds. Differences in vibration patterns keep a person's voice from sounding like a scraping chair or a sonic boom. These differences also serve to keep two different people from sounding alike. In fact, differences in vibration patterns enable us to differentiate the vowels, consonants, intonations, and so forth used by only one person. Every different sound, then, has its own unique pattern of vibrations.

The trick in sound recording is to make a copy of these vibrations on a piece of recording tape so they can be heard again. The trick is performed in this way: As patterns of vibrating air enter the recorder's microphone, they are *translated* into *equivalent* patterns of vibrating *electrical* signals. These patterned electrical vibrations do not have much strength, but after they travel through the amplifier in the recorder, they are magnified. The magnified vibration patterns go on to the recording head which *prints* these patterns magnetically onto the tape as it passes by. Essentially, this is what is involved in the record function; the playback function is the reverse of recording.

During playback, the patterns of magnetic vibrations printed on the tape pass by the head of the recorder. The head *reads* the patterns on the tape and sends them to the amplifier to be magnified. From there the strengthened electrical vibrations travel to the speaker (a kind of reverse microphone) which *translates* them back into *equivalent* patterns of *air* vibrations which we perceive as sound.

While this basic process is found in all tape recorders, differences in sound reproduction among recorders can be attributed partially to the quality of components in the recording system and partially to the efficiency of the system as a whole. In the next section, we will examine the main component of the system, the head.

The Head. Heads, as we have noted, can print and read. They can also erase. These three activities compose the principal functions of heads. Some machines have a separate head for each function, but most machines have only two heads: one for erase, the other for playback and record.

When recording, two functions are normally at work: erasing and recording. The tape is ordinarily cleaned of any magnetic

patterns (erasing function) before new material is laid down
(recording function). In order for the erase head to contact
the tape before any recording is done, this head is located on
the feed-reel side of the record head. In playback, the erase
head is inoperative. Only the playback head, which may or may
not be the same as the record head, is active.

If we were to open up any one of the heads of the recorder,
we would find it shaped like a small horseshoe with the two tips
nearly touching each other. In order for the machine to record,
play back, or erase, these tips must touch the tape. If we are
recording, the erase head sends a strong current across its tips
to demagnetize the iron particles on the tape. Then the patterns of electrical vibrations from the machine turn the
horseshoe-shaped record head into a small electromagnet which
produces very small magnetic patterns on the freshly demagnetized tape as the tape passes by. This is the *printing* process.
When we play back the recording, the small magnetic patterns on
the tape create electrical vibration patterns in the playback
head. This is the *reading* process.

The quality of a head depends on how close the tips come to
each other. The space between the tips is called the *gap*. For
its function, the erase head has the widest gap of all heads.
Next in order, the record head should have a slightly wider gap
than the playback head in order to deliver the best performance.

This fact about record and playback gaps is responsible for
a surprise we may get on playing old tape recordings. Recorders
of some years ago did not have the ultranarrow gaps we find
today. In many cases, however, excellent quality was in fact
recorded by the older wide-gap heads, but the playback heads of
that day could not retrieve it. It took the advances of present-
day head-gap technology in order to appreciate from his tapes
what the earlier recordist could only appreciate live.

While the ideal seen in the professional and semi-professional
machines is to have separate heads for recording and playback
purposes, most recorders use the same head for both functions.
The gap width of a record/playback head is therefore a compromise. A compromise at this point, however, does not indicate
poor quality. Many very good quality recorders have only one
playback/record head. Good quality is the result of advancements in head construction. New materials have been developed
which make head surfaces harder than ever before. Ferrite heads
molded as a unit wear about one-tenth as fast as laminated per-
malloy heads under the same conditions. With the harder material, not only are narrower and more precisely formed gaps
possible, but the gaps will maintain their uniform dimensions
against wear far beyond what older head gaps could tolerate.

In the decision for or against separate playback and record
heads, more than the quality of reproduction must be considered.
At the present state of the industry, the availability of separate heads exists almost exclusively among open-reel recorders.
Among these recorders, separate heads offer versatility which
may or may not be important to your needs. First, the gaps of
the heads can be optimally designed for their respective functions. Second, it is possible to monitor what has been recorded
as it is being recorded. Third, special mixing and echo effects
are available to the recordist if the recorder is wired accordingly. These various points are considered later in this
chapter.

  TIP: The presence of more than two heads generally indicates quality. An instrument with only two heads, however,
  is not necessarily inferior.

Frequency Response. Frequency response has a lot to do with
the quality of a recorder. But frequency response figures can
be very misleading unless you know what to look for when reading
a recorder specification sheet. In this section, we will try to
indicate what you should look for any why and how it relates to
the recording you do. Certain questions will help us explore
this area.

  1. What is frequency response? We have said that sound is
made up of patterns of vibrations. Technicians refer to one
vibration as a cycle. They have made instruments capable of
counting the number of vibration cycles in a particular pattern.
They measure these patterns in terms of how many vibration
cycles occur in one second of sound or how many *cycles per
second, cps.*

  Some sounds, for example, high pitched musical notes, have
many thousands of vibration cycles per second in their patterns.
Other sounds like those heard from the low end of the piano key-
board have only a very few cycles per second. Between these
extremes, there are thousands of sounds whose patterns can be
measured. The range of vibration cycles or pitches that a tape
recorder head can record and play back accurately is called the
frequency response. It is written as a range by stating the
two ends of the range, for example, 50 cps-15,000 cps.

  The standard term for cycle per second is *Hertzocycle*, or
simply *Hertz*, abbreviated *Hz*. Although cycle per second is a
more descriptive term for the measurement of vibration patterns,
the recording industry has adopted Hertzocycle as the conventional term for expressing frequency response. Thus, the range
quoted above will be seen more often as 50 Hz-15,000 Hz or
50 Hz-15 KHz, where K stands for one thousand.

2. Can I depend on the frequency response quoted? How accurate is it? This is a crucial question because a quoted response may not tell the complete story and may even tell a false story.

The ideal recording head will reproduce a range of sound vibrations and play it back at the same relative volume as the original had. What happens, however, is that across that range, the strength of reproduction will vary slightly, and at the two ends of the range, it falls off sharply. For this reason, reputable manufacturers include in their frequency response specifications an indication of how faithfully the recorder reproduces all the pitches within a particular frequency response range, that is, how much variation in strength is present across the range. Variation in strength is measured in *decibels, db.*[4] For example, a frequency response may be stated as follows:

40 Hz-13,000 Hz ±3 db at 7 1/2 ips

This statement may be read: At the speed of 7 1/2 ips, the record or playback head is capable of reproducing a range of sound from 40 Hz to 13,000 Hz with only three decibels of variation either stronger or weaker than the original sound.[5] If the range were stated simply as 40 Hz-13,000 Hz at 7 1/2 ips, there is no way to know how much of that range represents *faithful* reproduction or even *audible* reproduction. For example, the decibel gain or loss may be so extensive at the extremes that only between 200 Hz-8,000 Hz does the recording resemble the original in relative strength. However, unless your normal operating conditions are like the optimum conditions under which the recorder was originally rated, you will not have available at every recording the full frequency response cited. As we shall see, these conditions can be approximated if not achieved.[6]

The question above may be answered: Yes, you can depend on the frequency response quoted provided it is a complete statement of frequency response containing the limits within which the range varies.

TIP: Two guidelines are important at this point. First, beware of recorders whose specifications omit the decibel variation. Second, for evaluating decibel variation where specified, this guide may be helpful: ±2 db or smaller is very good, ±3 db is good, ±4 db is average.

3. What frequency response is adequate for my needs? The answer to this question depends on whether you are interested in recording *voice only* or *both voice and music,* and what quality you want in your recording.

A keen human ear can hear a range of sound from about 20 Hz to 20,000 Hz. While the human voice does not span that wide a range, music may create vibrations even wider than this range. The fundamental tones of speech range roughly between 100 and 1,000 Hz. For most musical instruments, the fundamental frequencies fall within the 200 to 2,000 Hz range. Below these ranges are the low notes on the organ, piano, and harp; above these ranges are the harmonic frequencies. Without the higher harmonic frequencies, both speech and music are lifeless, booming, and decidedly irritating--the effect known as listener fatigue. Harmonics in the 3,000 to 7,000 Hz range give voices their clear and distinctively recognizable quality. Harmonic tones above 7,000 Hz add brilliant, life-like realism to both speech and music.

It is evident, then, that your interest, whether voice only or voice and music, will make a difference in how wide a frequency response will be needed. This difference in range for voice versus music has two important implications for you as a recorder buyer. First, you must be sure to purchase a recorder which has a range equal to your needs. That is, at top speed the frequency response should be sufficiently wide to reproduce the quality needed. What should that frequency response be?

TIP: *Category I:* If good voice reproduction is all that is necessary, look for a frequency response of about 100 Hz-8,000 Hz ±3 db or ±4 db at fastest speed.

Category II: If very good voice reproduction and uncritical music reproduction is desired, look for a frequency response of about 50 Hz-10,000 Hz ±3 db at fastest speed.

Category III: If very good voice and very good music reproduction are required, look for a frequency response of about 50 Hz-15,000 Hz ±2 db or wider at fastest speed.[7]

The second implication of frequency response and recording content is that you should record your material at a speed appropriate to the quality desired. It is important to realize that the frequency response narrows as the speed gets slower. It is for this reason that the specifications of a three-speed recorder may show a frequency response for each speed similar to the following:

> 30 Hz-14,000 Hz at 7 1/2 ips
>
> 50 Hz-8,500 Hz at 3 3/4 ips
>
> 50 Hz-6,000 Hz at 1 7/8 ips

Suppose you had purchased such a machine, basing your decision about frequency response on the fact that 30 Hz-14,000 Hz

at 7 1/2 ips would provide a sufficiently wide range for any expected musical uses (see Category III above). It would be wise,
then, to use the other speeds to record material for which highest quality was not prerequisite. Thus, 3 3/4 ips might be used
for the quality of reproduction found in Category II above, and
1 7/8 ips for the quality of Category I. This kind of judgment
constitutes the wisest use of speed for tape economy and recording quality.

4. What does frequency response mean to me in terms of recorder cost? As emphasized throughout this chapter, no one
should buy a recorder on the basis of one specification alone.
The single feature approach, however, has been the strategy of
some recorder manufacturers who have promoted frequency response
as the key indicator of quality. It is not. The danger in this
sales strategy is that the accompanying transport system components may not equal the quality of the heads. Without comparable quality in all components, the distressing effect is
that the frequency response quoted can never be appreciated.
The proper exercise of caution is to evaluate a recorder on more
than one specification.

In sum, to gain the maximum from increased frequency response
capability, the quality of other features should also increase
to the same level. Just which specifications fall in different
quality categories is provided in the summary chart, Figure 2,
on page 32.

Volume and Tone Controls. Adjusting the record (input) and
the playback (output) functions of a recorder is accomplished
through the volume and tone controls in conjunction with the
record level monitor.

1. Input Control. The input control is used during the recording process to allow a maximum amount of volume to be delivered to the tape without distortion. Any kind of volume control approach should be able to distinguish, for the eye or
automatically, between *safe* and *distort* volume.

There are two principal ways in which input volume can be
controlled: (1) manually and (2) automatically. There are ordinarily two related recorder components needed to control the
input volume manually. The first is a *volume control knob* by
which greater or lesser volume is obtained. The second component is an *indicator* which registers how much volume is present.

There are three common types of input indicators: meter,
magic eye, and neon bulb. Because fine volume adjustments will
register on them, the first two are the most accurate indicators
of recording level.

There are great differences in VU (volume unit) meters, and
the meters on most home equipment are not the precision instruments of the professional recordist. A professional VU meter
has exacting specifications by which the recordist knows precisely the response time of the needle to an increase in sound
and the amount the needle will overshoot the actual level of
that sound. The home recorder meter sometimes is not even calibrated and if calibrated does not operate in a carefully controlled manner. Since the recordist really does not know when
he is overloading and distorting the recording or underrecord-
ing, he simply has to get used to the characteristics of each
meter and rely on some luck.

The magic eye is an instantaneous and accurate indicator.
While superior to the ordinary nonprofessional VU meter in use-
fulness, the magic eye is not found often on current equipment
in preference to the more professional look of the VU indicator.

The neon bulb, which usually has a normal side and a distort
side, provides only a gross indication of input volume. The
normal side glows as long as the volume is not distorting. When
the volume is excessive, the distort side of the bulb lights up.
This indicator is rarely used now.

The second method of control, the automatic volume control,
requires no attention from the operator. In many recorder
models, the volume control knob is inoperative while the automatic control is engaged, and no visual indicator is necessary.
Not only is distorting volume reduced, but weak volume is somewhat boosted. There are many machines on the market which offer
both the manual and the automatic record level controls.

TIP: The automatic volume control is primarily of value for
voice recordings. It may distort music by cutting off loud
peaks and boosting soft parts. If music is on your recording agenda, be sure to have a manual adjustment (volume knob
plus indicator) on the machine you use. The manual adjustment is also necessary for good quality voice recordings,
since the noise level increases whenever there is a pause
in the voice.

2. Output Control. The sound coming from the recording tape
out through the speaker may be adjusted in two ways: in volume
and in tone. Volume control is found on all machines, but not
tone control. However, the latter is an important asset in
playing back music.

Tone control is a manual adjustment which, by filtering out
certain portions of the frequency range, has the effect of emphasizing bass or treble response. An adjustment of tone away

from treble toward bass suppresses high frequencies; it does not actually augment bass frequencies. Thus, tone adjustments away from treble narrow the frequency response range just as if the recorder did not have heads with wider capabilities.

Tone quality is difficult to evaluate without making some comparisons between recorders. Unfortunately, recorder specifications offer no help here. In actual recorder shopping, after you have narrowed the choice of machines, take a tape with pre-recorded sections of voice and slow music to the dealer. Play the tape on the machine while adjusting the tone controls. Compare the tonal range and the naturalness of tone. Then, using the machines in question, record a segment of music and voice to make the same kinds of comparisons.

On the better AC/DC recorders, both open reel and cassette, the record level indicator also serves as a battery condition indicator. It is ordinarily possible to check the total battery charge during playback. Without this type of provision, it is difficult to know whether the strength of the batteries is sufficient for the job ahead or whether the batteries should be replaced or recharged.

TIP: We recommend that an AC/DC machine without a battery condition indicator be rejected. The best indicator is one that can be monitored at any time. The second best indicator uses a light or a buzzer which is activated when batteries are nearly exhausted.

Signal-to-Noise Ratio. One measure of the quality of the electrical recording system is expressed in terms of a ratio. Over and above the sound intended for recording, the electrical functioning of every recorder tends to put a small amount of sound of its own on the tape. The magnetic characteristics of tape oxide also contribute a bit of sound (called hiss) in addition to what comes from the recorder. The unwanted sounds are referred to as noise; the wanted target sound is known as signal. By using a measuring instrument, technicians can tell how much undistorted signal the recorder can produce in relation to the noise in the recording. This measurement is expressed in decibels. For example, if there are 40 db of signal to 1 db of noise, that is, 40/1, then the signal-to-noise ratio is 40 db. Another way of referring to the signal-to-noise ratio is in terms of *dynamic range:* A recorder with 40 db signal-to-noise ratio has a dynamic range of 40 db.

When cassette recorders first appeared, they displayed notoriously low signal-to-noise ratios (loud hiss). Slow speed, narrow tracks, and less than the best electronics worked to keep the cassette from becoming a high fidelity medium. Open-reel

recorders have not been seriously affected by these problems:
Fast speeds and quality electronics are available, and even at
their narrowest, open-reel tracks are wider than cassette tracks.

In order to bring cassette recorders into the realm of high
fidelity, an all-out attack on hiss was launched. It yielded
several important breakthroughs. Two lines of attack have been
used, one for each source of hiss, the recorder and the tape.
In cassette recorders, speed and track widths are standardized,
but better electronics and superior heads have measurably improved the dynamic range of these recorders. Most significant
for hiss reduction, however, are the noise suppressing systems.
For cassette tape, there are better coating materials and application techniques. The combination of improvements puts cassette signal-to-noise ratios on a technical par with those of
the best open-reel recorders.

A discussion of tapes will be reserved for Chapter 5; here we
will look at the noise suppression systems. There are several
different systems on the market, but the most common one, the
Dolby Type B, will be briefly described below. Most major recording companies use this system for their prerecorded tapes,
and a large number of recorder manufacturers have licenses to
incorporate the Dolby into their tape units. The Dolby system
is standardized so that any Dolbyized tape can be used with any
Dolby suppressor, whether the unit is built into a recorder or
is external.

To sketch the principle underlying the Dolby system, we begin
by observing that hiss is most noticeable when the recorded material is low in volume and high in frequency. The inventor,
Ray Dolby, developed a piece of equipment which boosts the volume
of high frequency content coming in from the microphone and records this exaggeration on the tape. At this time, of course,
hiss is recorded as well. When the system is used in reverse
for playback, the exaggeration is reduced in volume to normal
levels, but in the process the hiss level is also decreased by a
comparable amount, taking it far below what it would be without
the system.

There are two major problems inherent in this system which
the recorder shopper should be aware of. One is the matter of
inter-recorder compatibility. For best results, a Dolbyized
tape should be used with a Dolby suppressor for playback. A
Dolby-processed tape, however, can be used on a non-Dolby recorder, but the tone control must be adjusted to reduce the
exaggerated treble (high frequencies). High frequencies can be
preserved only by means of Dolby playback. Another problem is
that the Dolby can do nothing for hiss already recorded on a
tape, since it operates only on sound before it is recorded.

These two problems, Dolby/non-Dolby incompatibility and ineffec-
tiveness for prerecorded material, have led to the development
of other systems to cope with hiss.

TIP: A signal-to-noise ratio (abbreviated S/N) figure, un-
altered by a noise suppression system, should appear in the
recorder specifications. If the ratio for a machine is between 40 db and 45 db, it is adequate for most uses involving speech. For music, 45 db to 50 db is adequate, and
50 db or above is superb for any kind of recording.

For the cassette recordist who is a perfectionist, a
noise suppression system may be worth the considerable investment, provided his recorder is good enough to show the
difference. It will increase the S/N ratio by about 5 db.
For AC/DC machines, noise suppressing devices are usually
the more costly external units. However, for most purposes
requiring good quality, a significant and generally adequate
improvement in dynamic range can be gained by simply choosing the right kind of tape. See Chapter 4 for a discussion
of tape characteristics.

Because many cassette recorder specifications omit the signal-
to-noise ratio, the shopper may be at a loss when trying to
evaluate quality at this point. There are some simple tests you
can use to arrive at a judgment.

When two machines are compared, switch the machines into record mode without inserting a cassette magazine. With your fin-
ger, keep the record-lock lever in the cartridge well from moving forward. Once in record mode, turn the volume controls all
the way up and monitor with headphones if possible. The noise
you hear from each machine is produced by the motor and electrical circuitry and is the noise that gets on the tape when recording. The recorder with the least amount of hiss by this
comparison will have the wider dynamic range.

A second test is usable for machines with record-monitoring
facilities (separate record and playback heads). In the store,
record some soft music by direct line from some source (e.g.,
FM radio or phonograph) simultaneously to the two recorders in
question. As the recording progresses, activate the speaker of
the source machine so the source material is audible. Then turn
the source speaker off and quickly activate the speaker of one
of the machines under test so that what has been recorded is
audible. By alternating back and forth between source and each
machine being tested, and between the two machines under test,
you will get a good idea of the level of background hiss in each
machine compared with the original sound.

When these tests are used in conjunction with tests related
to the effect of tape types on hiss (mentioned on p. 92), it is
difficult to go wrong in your evaluation of record and playback
quality.

To summarize, the principal factors affecting recording
quality have been examined. It may be helpful to see the recommendations listed according to categories of quality (Figure 2).

Feature	Category I Good Voice Reproduction	Category II Very Good Voice, Uncritical Music Reproduction	Category III Very Good Voice, Very Good Music Reproduction
Wow and Flutter	.25-.20%	.20-.15%	.15 or less
Frequency Response	At least 100 Hz- 8,000 Hz ±4 db at fastest speed	About 50 Hz- 10,000 Hz ±3 db at fastest speed	30 Hz- 15,000 Hz ±2 db or wider at fastest speed
Volume Control	AVC without manual control is sufficient	AVC is sufficient, manual better for music	Manual essential for voice and music
Signal-to- Noise Ratio	40 db-45 db	45 db-50 db	50 db or greater

Fig. 2.   Summary of Recorder Specifications by Category

HOW MANY TRACKS SHOULD THE RECORDER HAVE?

One common way to refer to tape recorders is with reference
to tracks: "He has a two-track machine." The term *track* is
also used in connection with recording tape: "I can play only
four-track tapes on my recorder." The meaning of these terms is
of central importance to the person planning to buy a recorder.
The following discussion of tracks will lead us to consider what
tracks are, how many are possible, how they are arranged, how

they relate to monophonic and stereophonic recording, what kinds
of track difficulties you can expect when purchasing a recorder,
and which track arrangement on a machine is best for you.

What Is a Track?

We have described the work of the record head as that of
printing vibrating electrical patterns on a tape as it passes by
the head. With reference to tape, a track is the path of magnetically printed patterns recorded on the tape. The statement,
"I can play only four-track tapes on my recorder," cannot be
said of blank tapes. Blank tape is *no-track* tape. Material
must be recorded on the tape by a four-track recorder before it
can be called four-track tape. With reference to a recorder, as
in "He has a two-track machine," track simply means the path a
recorder is capable of laying down on the tape it uses. A two-
track recorder, then, is one capable of recording a maximum of
two paths on a piece of tape.

It should be clearly understood that all the tracks are recorded on only one side of the tape, the coated side. When the
recorder operator turns the tape over, he is not actually using
both front and back (coating and backing) of the recording tape.
When the tape is turned over, it is only the tape reels that are
reversed; the same coated side of the tape remains in contact
with the recorder heads. Reels are often marked *side one* or
side two, but side one of the reel gives the heads access to
only one portion of the tape coating. Side two of the reel
gives access to a different portion of the same coating side.

How Many Tracks Are Possible?

The number and construction of recorder heads determine the
number of tracks possible for a given machine. Some heads are
designed to produce only one wide track of recording on the tape.
Machines so equipped are known as full-track recorders and are
used for very special purposes, as in making movie sound tracks.
The majority of heads can record two tracks of material on the
same tape. Such machines may be referred to as two-track, dual-
track, or half-track recorders. The second most frequent number
of tracks is four. Machines with this capability are called
four-track or quarter-track recorders. Eight tracks on a single
length of tape are found on continuous-loop cartridge machines
and open-reel quadraphonic (four-at-a-time record and playback)
recorders. Commercial machines, as used in recording studios,
may produce as many as two dozen tracks simultaneously.

In the following discussion, our attention will center on
two-track and four-track open-reel and cassette recorders. One-
and eight-track machines do not ordinarily serve the general

needs of the language recordist. Special needs, however, such
as recording four simultaneous and discrete channels of natural
group interaction, may call for a reconsideration of the eight-
track reel-to-reel recorder. The principles of eight-track
operation can be derived easily from the following pages. Aside
from such special uses, eight-track machines are primarily media
for quadraphonic music.

The recordings produced by any of these machines, whether
open reel or cassette, two track or four track, bear a simi-
larity: All the tracks are numbered in the same way. Track one
is always on the track position closest to the top edge of the
tape during the first pass of the tape across the heads from
left to right. The recording of a track on a tape establishes
the track numbering for that tape, because the width of the
track indicates how many positions can be fitted on the coating.
After the first track is recorded, track positions are numbered
consecutively down the tape with the largest track number
closest to the bottom edge. Once the numbering is fixed, it
does not change regardless of which track position may be filled
next. Track numbering is not based on the order in which the
tracks are recorded.

Monophonic and Stereophonic Track Arrangements

As we have mentioned, tape recorders may be designated according to the *number* of tracks the head can print or read.
This distinction gives us two track and four track. Recorders
are also referred to by channels, the number of tracks that can
be recorded or played *at the same time*. This distinction gives
us monophonic (mono or one channel) and stereophonic (stereo or
two channel).[9] A mono recorder is one that handles only one
track at a time; a stereo recorder handles two (or more) at a
time. Figure 3 illustrates the combinations to be discussed
here.

TOTAL NUMBER OF TRACKS POSSIBLE

			Two	Four
N C		One	Two-Track Mono	Four-Track Mono
U H M A O B N F E N R E L S		Two	Two-Track Stereo	Four-Track Stereo

Fig. 3. Common Track Arrangements

Two-Track Monophonic Recorders. Two-track mono recorders
come in both open-reel and cassette varieties. The track arrangement for both is identical, although track width is different. Open-reel recorders use recording tape which is one-
fourth-inch wide, while cassette magazines contain tape which is
about one-eighth inch in width. Cassette tracks are consequently narrower than open-reel tracks.

In two-track mono recording, the head gap contacts the upper
half of the tape width (track one) during the first pass of the
tape from the supply reel to the take-up reel (Figure 4). When
the tape or magazine has been reversed, track one becomes the
lower track. The upper half of the tape (track two) may then be
filled with recording. The recording head remains immobile. It
is because the head gap is off-center on the vertical axis with
respect to the tape that the reversed tape can provide the new
area for recording. A narrow *gutter* or *guard band* or unrecorded
strip is left between the two tracks and along the edges of the
coating.

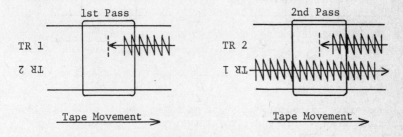

Fig. 4. Two-Track Monophonic Tracking

Four-Track Monophonic Recorders. In four-track mono recording, the open-reel recorder differs from the cassette in both
arrangement and width of tracks. With both, however, twice as
much recording can be put on a length of tape as is possible
with a two-track recorder.

Open-reel mono machines record their tracks one at a time in
the following order: one, four, three, two. On the first two
passes of the tape across the recording head, the head remains
in the same position. Pass one puts track one on the tape; pass
two lays down track four (Figure 5). For the third and fourth
passes, either the head is moved to a new vertical position or a
second head at that position is activated. Pass three records
track three, and pass four delivers track two. The effect of
this arrangement is that adjacent tracks are recorded in opposite directions. A narrow guard band is still present between
each pair of tracks and perhaps along the edges of the tape.

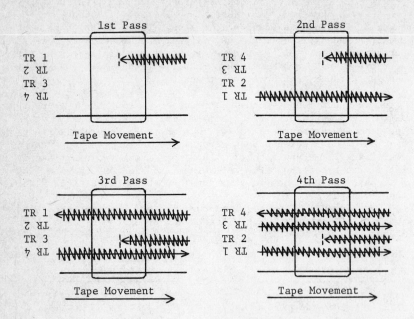

Fig. 5. Four-Track Monophonic Open-Reel Tracking

Four-track monophonic cassette machines record their tracks
in this order: one, four, two, three, with the result that
tracks one and two run in one direction and tracks three and
four run in the opposite direction (Figure 6). Four-track monophonic cassette recorders are found almost exclusively in special
audio-visual applications, as in sound-with-sound language
laboratory facilities or in portables which simulate those
features.

Four-Track Stereophonic Recorders. In stereo recording, two
vertically aligned head gaps must be used simultaneously. In
general, the more gaps per head, the greater the cost to the recorder purchaser. Since two tracks are recorded at the same
time by a four-track stereo machine, the same amount of recording
time is available on one reel of tape as is available on the
same reel in a two-track mono format at the same speed. A two-
track recorder uses up the tape in two passes; likewise, a four-
track stereo recorder.

As in mono recording, the open-reel and cassette stereo machines differ from each other in both arrangement and width of
tracks. The open-reel recorder uses the same alternating-
direction arrangement as seen in its four-track monophonic

counterpart. For stereo, tracks one and three are produced together on the first pass. The reels are reversed, then tracks
four and two are recorded on the second pass without any movement of the recorder heads. See Figure 7, tape type three, for
an illustration of a tape recorded in this way. The top track
in each pass (track one or track four) is called the left channel;
the lower track (track three or track two) is called the right
channel.

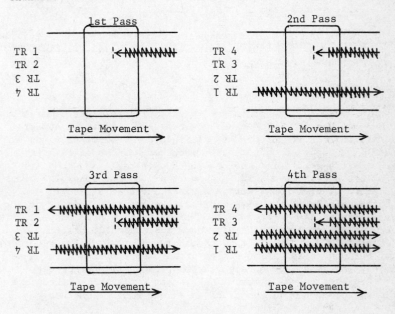

Fig. 6. Four-Track Monophonic Cassette Tracking

The one-three, four-two stereo tracking pattern is a permanent
reminder of a period in tape recorder history when head technology was not sufficiently advanced to permit two adjacent
tracks to be recorded simultaneously. This format creates many
compatibility problems to be pointed out below. Happily, tech-
nological progress has allowed cassette recorders to use the
adjacent-track format, thereby eliminating almost all compatibility problems.

The stereo cassette machine records its tracks so that the
end result is the parallel formation seen in its monophonic
counterpart. Tracks one and two, then tracks four and three are
recorded. Figure 8, tape type three, shows what such a
recording arrangement looks like.

Four-track stereo recorders are marketed primarily for stereo music fans. But they are also of interest to the language recordist. As an example, in many situations two individuals are being recorded, whether in an interview or supplying different voices for a taped language drill. For top quality recording of each participant, while avoiding the problems of orienting a single microphone so that it will pick up both voices well, two microphones can be used, one for each channel. There are other uses of the stereo format to be discussed in Chapters 6 and 7.

Two-Track Stereophonic Recorders. Two-track stereos are found in some language laboratory equipment. The characteristics of these machines are discussed below.

Tracking Compatibility among Recorders

Before buying a recorder, it is essential to understand what it can and cannot do. Because of the great variety of numbers, widths, and formats of tracks, all recorders cannot play and erase tape recorded on all other machines. First of all, this means that a recorder cannot use both open reels and cassette magazines unless it has two transport systems or some kind of elaborate adapter. Cassette magazines and open reels are not interchangeable on the same machine. Second, the variety of track formats has created further compatibility problems. All open-reel recorders cannot play back and erase all tracking arrangements of open-reel tape. Neither can all cassette recorders play back and erase all tracking arrangements of cassette magazines. The head gaps of a particular recorder, whether open-reel or cassette, must match the tracks on the prerecorded tape it uses, or there will be problems of one kind or another.

Open-Reel Recording. To illustrate the dimensions of this problem graphically, we have chosen the four most common track arrangements on open-reel tape. We have then asked the question: Which of these types of tape can be played as they were recorded when using the four most common types of open-reel recorders: two-track mono, four-track stereo, four-track mono, and four-track mono/stereo? For example, can a stereo tape be played back stereophonically on a mono recorder? Can a stereo recorder play back a mono recording monophonically? For erasing, the question is simply: Can one recorder remove all the signal on a tape recorded by another machine? Figure 7 shows the permissible combinations.

Recorder Types

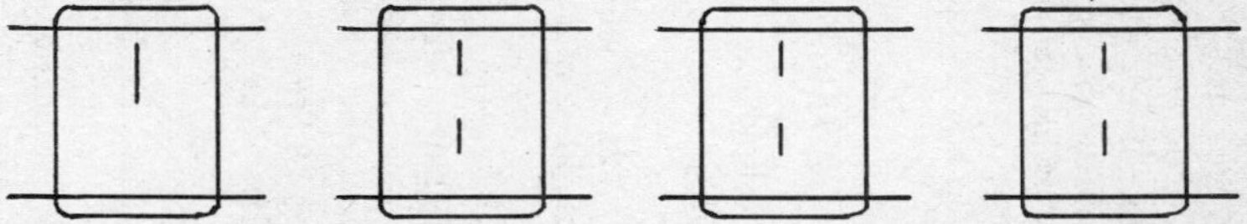

Tape Types

Tape recorded on:	2-track mono		4-track stereo		4-track mono		4-track mono/stereo	
	Play	Erase	Play	Erase	Play	Erase	Play	Erase
1. Tracks 1 and 2 with a 2-track mono recorder	YES	YES	NO	NO	YES	NO	YES	NO
2. Tracks 1 and 4 with a 4-track mono recorder	YES	YES	YES	YES	YES	YES	YES	YES
3. Tracks 1 and 3, 2 and 4 with a 4-track stereo recorder	NO	YES	YES	YES	NO	YES	YES	YES
4. Tracks 1,2,3,4 with a 4-track mono recorder	NO	YES	YES	YES	YES	YES	YES	YES

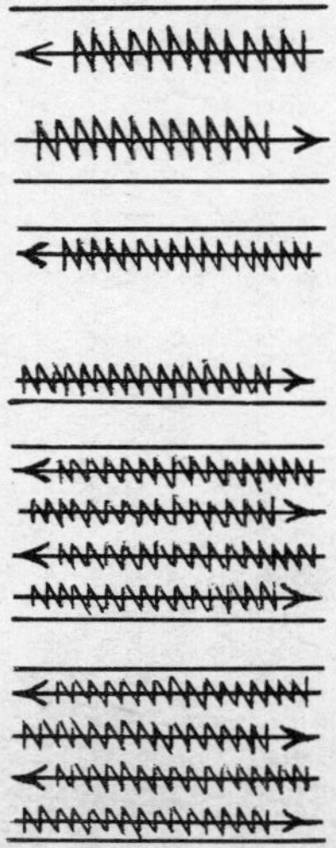

Fig. 7. Open-Reel Recorder and Tape Tracking

Erasing difficulties are created when the four-track erase
head cannot reach the guard band in which sound remains from two-
track recording. Playback difficulties are created when the two-
track playback head picks up more than one track of material at
the same time, and when the four-track mono head cannot play both
stereo tracks at the same time. When the four-track stereo head
picks up more than one track, the playback volume control of one
channel can be turned to zero so that only one track is audible.

If the machine you intend to purchase is an open-reel recorder
for voice-only or voice and music needs, the following TIPS may
guide your selection.

TIP: A. If you are not interested in stereo music (either
because mono music is acceptable or because you have voice-
only interests), then either a two- or a four-track mono
recorder may suit your needs. (Neither of these machines
can play four-track stereo tapes.)

1. Two-track mono. Because most voice-only tapes are made
    on the popular two-track recorder, this may be an im-
    portant consideration. This recorder will not be able
    to play a tape on which all four tracks are recorded by
    a four-track mono recorder; two tracks only, one and
    four, present no problems.

2. Four-track mono. A four-track mono recorder will allow
    you to get twice the amount of recording on a reel of
    tape as is possible with a two-track mono machine. How-
    ever, the recorder will not be able to erase a two-track
    tape completely.[10] If you want to erase an entire tape,
    a bulk eraser is the best device to use. See Chapter 2
    for suggestions on purchasing and using bulk erasers.

B. If you are interested in stereo music in addition to
voice recording or in the applications of stereo for language
recording, a four-track mono/stereo recorder is the most versatile machine for your needs. This combination of stereo
and mono allows for recording with much tape economy. The
recorder can handle almost any tape type. A bulk eraser can
offset the recorder's inability to fully erase a tape recorded on a two-track recorder. This inability may be minor,
as suggested in the note above. Unfortunately, this ideal
tracking combination for the language recordist is not available in many recorders primarily because the industry is
geared to the stereo and quadraphonic music enthusiast.

Cassette Recording. A chart similar to that prepared for
open-reel recorders may also be used to highlight points of compatibility and incompatibility among various cassette recorders

and tape formats. One machine, called a four-track stereo/two-track mono, does not use a true two-track head for two-track mono. Rather, mono recording is achieved by letting both stereo head gaps record the same material at the same time. The four-track mono/stereo permits the activation of head gaps singly or in pairs. This is a feature restricted to language laboratory needs and is not readily available in portable models. As shown in Figure 8, the two erase problems occur with four-track machines which are unable to reach the guard band of sound remaining from a true two-track recording. The playback problem results when the two-track recorder picks up two tracks of different material at the same time. The picture is one of greater overall compatibility, a key virtue of the cassette system insisted on by the licensing company, Philips-Norelco.

If you are interested in purchasing a cassette recorder for your voice-only or voice and music needs, the recommendations below may help.

TIP: The recorders in Figure 8 are listed in a generally ascending order of price from left to right.

A. If you are interested in voice recording only, the two-track mono cassette is probably the best all-round choice.

B. As among open-reel machines, the most versatile arrangement is the four-track mono/stereo. It gives stereo capability when needed and tape economy through single-track mono. Unfortunately, machines of this type are difficult to find. If tape economy is less important than recorder price, the four-track stereo/two-track mono is the best compromise. In either case, a bulk eraser will be required to completely erase any two-track tapes if the need arises.

Special Track Features

Two features involving simultaneous playback and record functions are available at extra cost on some recorders.

Sound-with-Sound. Sound-with-sound is a feature found in some language laboratories and on some expensive home models. This feature requires what may be called a modified two-track or four-track stereo recorder. It must be stereo because two heads and two tracks are used at the same time. It must be modified so that one of the two tracks may play back at the same time the other track is recording. In the language laboratory, the student plays the prerecorded tape, listening to the model's voice on one track through the headset. A second track is activated for recording the student's responses through his microphone. For comparison purposes, the student rewinds the tape, puts both heads in playback mode (or activates a playback head on his track), and listens to the model's voice and his own responses.

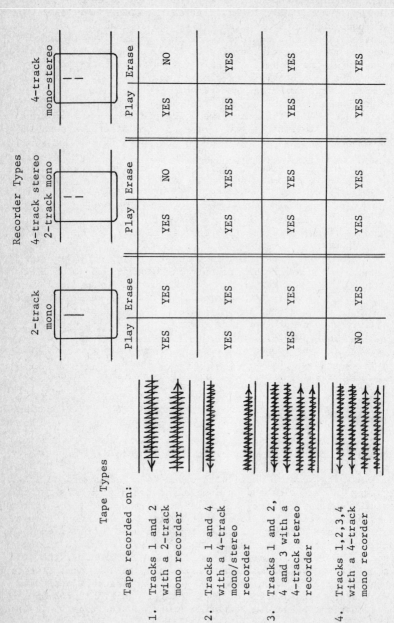

Fig. 8. Cassette Recorder and Tape Tracking

Sound (the student's voice) is *with* sound (the model's voice) in the sense that the two voices are on separate tracks and can be heard at the same time.

In order to make tapes for sound-with-sound operation, it is not necessary to record these tapes on a sound-with-sound recorder. The only requirement is to record the voice of the model with a monophonic recorder using track one of a two-track recorder or tracks one and four of a four-track recorder.

Sound-with-sound can be used to create a special echo effect by recording on a second track (the right channel) exactly the same material which is on another track (the left channel). Since the record gap is horizontally to the left of the playback gap, the second track is recorded on the tape slightly behind the first track. When played back with two vertically aligned head gaps, the physical separation of the same material appears as a temporal delay—the echo.

Sound-on-Sound. A refined variation of sound-with-sound is found on some four-track stereo recorders. This feature permits an accurate mixing of two voices on a single track, a technique not possible using sound-with-sound equipment.

A recording is made on one track. As it is played back, a person may speak, sing, or otherwise introduce sound along with the sound he hears. As this new material is recorded on a second track, the original sound is also recorded onto the same second track. Thus, a blend of original and new material is produced on one track. When the second track is played back, both recordings are heard. If the end product is not as desired, the original material is still available in order to rerecord the sound-on-sound track. Some recorders permit repeated cross-feeding from track to track. Others can put sound on sound only one time.

Provided on some machines is an echo button which connects the playback head with the record head of the same track. Recording then makes a cycle: record head to playback head, then back again to the record head, and so on. The physical distance between heads, discussed above under sound-with-sound, supplies the echo-like delay.

Sound (the second recording) is *on* sound (the original recording) in the sense that both voices have been mixed on the same track.

Sound-on-sound is a technique for creating special effects or for producing programs by combining various sound sources. Some language laboratory equipment incorporates this feature.

Record Monitoring

Whenever separate record and playback heads are used, there exists the possibility of hearing through the playback head the same material just recorded at the record head. Many manufacturers wire their recorders in such a way as to make this possibility available.

The most obvious advantage of this feature is that the recordist can check on the quality of his recording and make necessary adjustments as he records, rather than afterwards. It also facilitates aligning playback and record heads should the need arise.

Many recorders have jacks through which you can listen to the sound during recording. What is being monitored is often simply the *input*, the original sound to be recorded. Record monitoring allows you to listen to the *output*, the sound of the input after being recorded on tape. The shopper should carefully distinguish between these two kinds of monitoring facilities.

The three features discussed in this section, sound-with-sound, sound-on-sound, and record monitoring, require separate record and playback head gaps. With open-reel recorders there has been no major obstacle to adding heads; with cassette recorders, this requirement has become a major challenge. Since the physical contours of cassette magazines are standardized, there is no room in which to fit another head. Progress is being made to put separate record and playback gaps in the same head and sufficiently close together to use the same pressure pad.

Until these developments are widely available, the shopper interested in any of these special features will be looking at open-reel recorders.

In summary, tracks are troublesome. They can be less troublesome if you choose either a very versatile instrument, an instrument which will meet the more limited track needs you may have, or two recorders with complementary tracking arrangements. Whatever the decision, understanding the whys and wherefores of tracks is essential to the choice you make. In this section, we have introduced the most important considerations involved in making the best decision.

HOW EASY TO USE AND HOW DURABLE IS THE RECORDER?

When you buy a tape recorder, you should be pleased not only with its capabilities, but satisfied with its usability and durability as well.

What Are Some of the Factors to Watch for in Usability?

Pause Control. One feature which makes the recorder easier to use, whether in recording or playback, is the pause control. It allows the operator to stop, pause, and begin again mid-course in playback or record operations without changing modes. This is an especially welcomed feature for recording such things as language drills and tape letters where short stops are often necessary. It is helpful, too, for playback for occasions such as using the recorder in the classroom, or to accompany slides, or to transcribe data from the tape.

Pause controls are of two varieties: a *mechanical pause* which acts as a brake on the transport system, and an *electrical pause* which affects the electrical power of the recorder. A mechanical pause will stop the reels more quickly than an electrical pause; thus, it is better for transcription and editing purposes. Most purely mechanical pauses provide a completely silent stop without affecting the recording at all. When it is more convenient for the operator to be at some distance from the machine or to have his hands free, as in classroom use, a foot pedal may be used.

Electrical pauses are good for stopping the recorder at a distance, hence the name *remote control*. They are typically built into a microphone, although on *split mikes* the pause can be separated conveniently for use away from the mike.[11] The speed with which the electrical pause stops the tape is a function of the tape speed being used. When the power is turned off, the reels must glide to a halt. The faster the tape speed, the longer it takes the reels to stop. At faster speeds, this can be a decided disadvantage for transcription and editing. At 1 7/8 ips or slower, the pause is nearly instantaneous.

Another drawback of the electrical pause occurs during recording. When the pause is activated or released while in record mode, the disturbance of the electrical functioning of the recorder generally leaves a pop on the tape.

TIP: Check the pause control for two points: speed in stopping tape movement and electrical interference during recording. Some mechanical pauses are tied into the electrical system, and some electrical pauses employ a mechanical braking device, as well. While the mechanical pause control is best for most language recording uses, the remote control facility is an asset in certain circumstances mentioned in Chapter 7. On some machines both pause types are available, but at least one or the other can be found on every size and type of recorder.

Digital Counter. Another convenient recorder feature which
facilitates recorder use is the digital counter (also called an
index counter). It is found even on the smallest pocket cassettes. A counter is helpful in locating specific sections on
a reel of tape.

On the tape box or housing, many recorder users make an inventory of the contents of a tape. Included opposite each entry
is the counter reading corresponding to that section, for example:

                    French nasalized vowels 000-127
                    French initial /ž/   128-319

To locate the second drill, the counter must first be set at
zero at the beginning of the reel. Then, fast forward is used
to speed the tape along until 128 registers on the counter.

Counters are ordinarily attached to either the feed reel or
the take-up reel spindle. As the tape moves, the counter tal-
lies the number of revolutions the reel makes, not the feet of
tape that pass by. The digital counter serves as only an approximate location guide. Because machines differ in the way
counter mechanisms are attached, different machines will produce
different readings for the same selection on a tape. Tightness
or looseness of tape windings will affect readings even on the
same recorder. The more revolutions needed to arrive at a section, the more inaccurate the reading is likely to be. Within
short lengths of tape, however, the counter can be very accurate.

For open-reel recorders, an accessory is available which is
mounted on the top surface of the machine so that it will contact the tape being pulled along by the capstan. The device
registers tape in feet and the equivalent amount of time in
hours and minutes. The tape timer operates when tape motion is
either forward or reverse. Besides its value in cueing, it is[12]
a useful aid when editing a tape to a certain program length.

Types and Locations of Controls. Ease of operation also reflects the types and locations of controls which are provided
and the placement of indicators. Some controls are the piano-
key type, others are sliderule-type levers, others are pushbut-
tons, and still others are knobs. Which do you like best? Are
they easy to get to in a hurry? Can you manipulate them quickly
without looking? Do they provide quick, smooth action with a
minimum of noise? Can you enter record mode with one hand, or
does the placement of the record lock (the safety device used to
avoid accidental recording) require you to use two hands? Indicators such as volume monitors should be conveniently located.
Are they easy to read at a glance? Are they made for the standing or sitting operator?

It would be a serious oversight to consider how smooth and easy the controls are to the touch without also paying attention to how gentle the controls are to the tape. Two tests of how gently the transport system treats the tape should be used on a recorder (especially if AC-only) before purchasing it.

First, record a steady tone on a one-hundred-foot section of 1/2-mil, non-tensilized recording tape. Put the tape on the machine, run it at fast forward, then put on the brake with the stop control. Play the tape to see if the tone is at all distorted. If it is, the mechanism is too rough on the tape, stretching it when bringing it to a halt. The same procedure should be tried with fast reverse. This test will tell you whether or not it is possible to use thin tape on the machine safely.

A second test is to operate all controls taking note of the tape tension between reels and across the recorder heads. There should be sufficient tension in all functions to keep the tape from being slack in the tape slot, getting out of place in relation to the heads and tape guides, or falling off an open take-up or feed reel.

TIP: In making decisions about ease of handling, two final TIPS should be mentioned: (1) Do a lot of comparative shopping; and (2) Do not let the salesman tell you how easily the recorder handles. Try it yourself.

How Can I Check on the Durability of a Recorder?

For any recorder, but particularly for one to be used abroad, this is a crucial question. It is also a question that is difficult to answer with complete satisfaction. However, some pointers may be offered.

First of all, there are two aspects to durability. One inquires about the sturdiness of the instrument both mechanically and electronically. The other aspect has to do with care. While some machines are sturdier than others, no machine can stand up long to misuse, neglect, or careless handling. This aspect is up to the user. The question we are asking in this section is up to the manufacturer, namely, how well will a machine hold up if given proper care?

Some indication of how durable the recording system might be is given in the phrase *solid state*. In simplest terms, solid state means that the circuitry is composed of semiconductor devices (diodes, transistors, rectifiers, and so forth) rather than tubes. Solid state components are rugged, practically unbreakable, and have unlimited life. Tubes share none of these characteristics.

For an evaluation of particular machines, a key source of reliable information is to be found in product reports published
in popular periodicals such as *Audio, High Fidelity, Stereo Review, Consumer Reports,* and *Consumer Research* (formerly *Consumer's Bulletin*).

Finally, recorder servicemen can be quite informative with
candid remarks about specific recorder brands, if not specific
machines. What can be learned from several servicemen will often repay the effort of making the inquiries.

Once a particular machine has been purchased, it is wise to
try it out thoroughly before going abroad. Guarantees are of
little value abroad.

Now that we have come to the end of the section on recorder
selection, it is clear that selecting a tape recorder is an individual matter. It is individual in that each person has a
unique group of requirements that his recorder must meet--a certain price range, particular conditions of use, and a range of
special needs. There is no one *right* tape recorder that can
meet everyone's budget, uses, and needs. The right recorder is
one that reflects and meets your individual requirements.

The demands you make of a recorder in terms of price and projected uses can be seen as a *set of requirements*. A tape recorder, as a collection of electronic and mechanical components,
can be seen as a *set of specifications*. The goal in selecting a
tape recorder is to make the best match possible between your
individual set of requirements and the set of recorder specifications which can meet those requirements.

In this chapter we have been suggesting implicitly a three-
step approach to recorder selection. First, it is important for
you to determine in some detail the relevant set of requirements
you will make of a recorder. To help you define that set, we
raised questions about your individual circumstances. Then, we
looked at recorder specifications to see which ones would best
meet the various requirements you may have. As we proceeded
from question to question, the special set of recorder specifications best suited to meet your individual and varied needs be-
gan to emerge. The final step--and the one that is left to you--
is to find the particular tape recorder which has the specifications closest to the ideal set you have put together. Because
the assortment of recorders now available is so wide, you can be
certain there is at least one recorder that will match your requirements satisfactorily. When the machine is found, it is that
machine that is right for you personally.

2 Tape Recorder Care

The length of time a tape recorder will function properly is determined partially by how well it is built. The life of a recorder is also determined by how well it is cared for. In order
to preserve its performance quality for many years, the recorder
must be handled with considerable care. Preventative maintenance is a happier task than paying for preventable repairs.

GENERAL MAINTENANCE

Dirt

One of the agents of greatest destruction in the recorder is
dust or dirt. When it is allowed to accumulate, even in minute
amounts, there may be problems. Grit in the bearings serves as
a damaging abrasive, eventually increasing wow and flutter and
assuring lower quality recordings. Carried by the recording
tape, dust particles scratch and wear away the recording heads,
destroying the critical tolerances built into the head gap.

TIP: Keep the recorder covered when not in use.

Humidity

High humidity environments present other destructive agents.
Fungus attacks rosin solder and may weaken, even break, electrical connections. Mildew may grow on wood or leather surfaces. And moisture often has a detrimental effect on rubber
parts.

   To combat the effects of high humidity, a number of options
are available. In order to protect the electrical system of the
recorder, a permanent seal may be put around those parts of the
system which are subject to damage by fungus. The dealer, manufacturer, or owner of a tape recorder may tropicalize the machine by coating the vulnerable parts with an antifungus preparation. The compounds needed for this treatment are readily
available and easily applied.[1] An alternative to this method is
to avoid fungus by keeping moisture entirely away from the recorder during storage. The recorder may be placed in an airtight container--a metal box, or a zippered polyethylene bag--
with a dehumidifying agent and a humidity indicator card. When
the agent, usually in small sacks, has absorbed its quota of
moisture, it should be removed and replaced with a dry sack.
The wet sack can be put into the oven to be dried for reuse. To
protect wood or leather parts of a recorder from mildew, those
parts may be rubbed or sprayed with liquid silicone. This preparation is sold by shoe repair shops for waterproofing and
stainproofing leather goods.

   If you anticipate being in a high-humidity area for an extended period, it would be wise to have extra rubber parts on
hand if they are not available locally. A recorder serviceman
can show you how a belt, pulley, and rubber roller can be replaced.

Lubrication

   Most machines come from the factory permanently oiled. Because even a small amount of oil on the wrong spot may cause
slippage and serious quality loss in recordings, any additional
lubricating of bearings should be done by an experienced recorder repairman. For sliding metal parts, however, a silicone
grease can be applied without danger.

Battery Leakage

   A special precaution should be taken for AC/DC recorders being used with dry cells. When the recorder is not in use for a
long period of time, the batteries should be removed. Otherwise, they should be checked regularly. If any leakage appears,
replace the batteries immediately. Leakage can damage the recorder extensively, even permanently. Although all batteries
are more prone to problems in hot, humid areas than in moderate
climates, this precaution is especially pertinent for batteries
purchased abroad.

Tape Speed

   True tape speed is a vital factor in producing good tape recordings. Tape speed variations can be of two types: long term
and momentary. Long-term inaccuracies are the result of tape
speeds creeping away from their standard ips settings. They can
slow down so gradually that the difference may not be noticed at
all. Momentary variations are wow and flutter. By contrast,
these deviations can be quite noticeable when listening to a recording.

   Because long-term speed changes may not be obvious, it is important to check from time to time to see how true the speeds
are. Any deviation should be corrected as soon as possible.

   To check on speed accuracy, a specially marked tape or fly-
wheel device (both called strobes) in conjunction with a light
can be used. Another highly effective, but less costly, speed-
testing method uses ordinary recording tape. Carefully measure
out 150 feet of tape and attach leader to both ends. With the
transport speed set for 7 1/2 ips, time the tape from beginning
to end. If the tape runs out before four minutes have passed,
the recorder speed is fast; if four minutes arrive before the
tape ends, the speed is slow. Good recorders should be within
two percent of standard speed.[2] A two-percent deviation in this
test means ±3 feet or ±4.8 seconds. If significant deviation
from the standard is found, the recorder should be taken to a
competent recorder serviceman for adjustment.

   The discovery and correction of a tape speed problem do
nothing to rectify recordings already made. A speed problem
can be damaging for field recordings which will be subjected to
instrumental analysis. The best solution for this problem is to
record a tuning fork tone at the beginning and end of each critical recording. On playback in an audio laboratory, a variable
speed recorder can be adjusted exactly to the speed of the original recording by reference to the frequency of the known tone.

   Momentary variation is the second kind of tape speed performance which must be considered. Some degree of wow and flutter
is found even in the most professional of equipment. There are,
however, factors which may increase wow and flutter above what
is inherent in the transport mechanism or the result of normal
wear. Several of these will be mentioned briefly as pointers
to conditions which should be checked if wow and flutter is
greater than normal: (1) uneven feeding of tape from the feed
reel due to adjacent layers of tape adhering to each other;
(2) a warped feed reel rubbing on the surface of the recorder;
(3) extra wide or unevenly slit tape (principally *white-box*
tape) binding on the tape guides; (4) gummy tape guide and/or

pressure pads; (5) any bit of oil on a belt, the capstan, or roller; and (6) flat spots or smooth places on the roller caus-ing a slight skipping in the tension.

Flat spots may be caused by leaving the rubber roller pressed against the capstan for long periods of time. This may happen when the recorder is turned off but not taken out of play or re-cord mode. If the flats do not disappear by running the machine in play without tape for a while, the roller should be replaced.

Travel

Even sturdy solid state instruments can be damaged by the rigors of rough travel. Heads may get out of alignment, weak-nesses in the mounting of components may show up, and critical adjustments throughout the machine may be altered. Unless you will be carrying the recorder in your hand, the leather or fab-ric case may not provide enough protection. It would be safer to prepare a well-padded box for your recorder--one that can ab-sorb the jostles of the journey as well as seal out dirt, dust, and excessive moisture.

HEAD MAINTENANCE

Recorder heads cannot receive too much care. Because much of the recording quality is produced by the heads, these should be the objects of greatest attention.

Head Demagnetizing

By turning into an electromagnet, the record head is able to record; it magnetizes because of incoming electricity. With time, however, the head may develop magnetism of its own, be-coming in effect a permanent magnet. When this happens, the re-cord head will begin to erase recorded signals (especially high frequencies) and put static on tapes during record and playback operations.

Residual magnetism collects when recording, when taking the recorder out of the record mode, when unplugging a patch cord or mike line while the machine is turned on, and when the re-corder is in contact with stray magnetic fields. To avoid some residual magnetism, connect or disconnect lines only when the machine is turned off. Also, do not use a bulk eraser close to the recorder (within six to eight feet) because of the strong magnetic field the eraser creates.

To remove the residual magnetism in the head, a special de-vice, appropriately called a head demagnetizer (or degausser), must be used. A very few recorders are equipped with built-in automatic head demagnetizers, but most units are purchased separately. One demagnetizer for cassettes is in the shape of a cassette magazine which can be inserted into the recorder and plugged in for operation. The more typical demagnetizer for cassette and open-reel recorders is a hand-held device with one or two narrow prongs which are exposed to magnetized surfaces. This small, inexpensive piece of equipment may be operated on AC or DC. Most DC models are designed to use the DC supply of the dashboard lighter socket.

TIP: Before using the hand-held demagnetizer, certain precautions should be taken. Your watch, as well as all recording tape, should be removed from the vicinity of the recorder.

The demagnetizer should be activated a few feet from the recorder, brought slowly toward the recorder, passed through the tape slot in front of the heads, capstan, and tape guides, then slowly removed and turned off at arm's length from the recorder. In order to avoid scratching the heads and guides with the bare metal pole pieces of the demagnetizer, the poles can be covered with one layer of cellophane tape. For best recording results, demagnetizing should be repeated once per week under normal use.

Cleaning Heads and Keeping Them Clean

The narrow air space in the head, the gap, which contacts the tape, is a ready depository for lint, tape oxide particles, dust, and adhesive gum from splices. When such material collects on the head and in the gap, even in small amounts, the magnetizing effect of the head on the tape is impaired. High frequencies will be shorted out and any accumulation of fine dust causing the slightest separation of tape from the head will produce drastic volume losses in both playback and record.

Heads get dirty principally because tape is dirty. Loose oxide not only fills the head gaps and packs into pressure pads, pinch roller and guides, but it also abrades metal surfaces, becoming, in fact, the main cause of head gap deterioration. To protect the heads, the object is to reduce all unnecessary tape-head contact. Intimate contact is necessary only for recording and playback functions. For other functions, certain measures can save the heads considerable exposure.

In fast forward and reverse, tape lifters keep the tape away from the heads. For the last function, tape erasure, several precautions can be taken depending on the circumstances. If a long portion of only one track is to be erased, the recorder erase head must be used (recorder in record mode; no microphone; volume at zero). In this case, a thin plastic shim can be inserted between the tape and the playback/record head while erasing. If a whole reel of tape is to be erased, a bulk eraser will save the heads a great deal of needless wear.

The bulk eraser is a powerful electromagnet that does for tape what the head demagnetizer does for metal recorder parts. On some models, the size of a cigar box, tape is exposed to a plate on the top surface. Other models are hand-held like an iron and passed over the tape. Regardless of the size or shape, the eraser can do more harm than good, unless it is operated properly.

TIP: The eraser should be operated at a distance (six to eight feet) from your recorder and other recording tape. Before turning on the magnet, remove your watch from the area.

To erase recording tape, the reel or cassette magazine must be brought into the magnetic field and rotated through the field by hand smoothly and no faster than two inches per second, 2 ips. If it is rotated more quickly or erratically, a whooshing sound will be left on the tape. Next, with the power still on, turn the tape over and rotate it in the opposite direction. Remove the tape slowly from the field (to a distance of about three feet) before turning off the power. If the power is shut off before removing the tape, a magnetic field will be imprinted on the tape that is so strong that it will be difficult to remove.

TIP: Not all bulk erasers are adequately powerful for the job, especially hand-held models. Before purchasing a bulk eraser, try it out in the store on some tapes you need to erase. Especially with cassette tape, some oxides are highly resistant to erasure.

Even with the best of care, heads will accumulate dirt. To clean away the deposit, the following simple procedure should be followed frequently. A cotton-tipped swab, or Q-tip, should be saturated with a special head-cleaning preparation. By rubbing the heads lightly, the cotton will loosen any debris. A dry swab can be used to carry away the loosened material. For good measure, the capstan, tape guides, and lifters should be cleaned in a similar manner. Care should be taken, however, not to get the fluid on the rubber roller. By rubbing the roller with a soft cloth, the discoloration of oxide can be removed. The solvent should not be used on pressure pads because it will tend to take the oxide deeper into the pads and will dissolve the adhesive which holds the pads in place.

Some instructions suggest common denatured or isopropyl alcohol for head cleaning. It can do no harm and is good to use in

the absence of special cleaning solvent. However, alcohol cannot dissolve some binder deposits. Carbon tetrachloride, on the
other hand, is too strong a solvent. It has been known to attack the cement between laminations of the head, leave a gummy
deposit behind, corrode the metal of the head, and even damage
the surrounding plastic housing material. The best answer is to
use the specially prepared solvent.

Pressure Pads

Many recorders employ pressure pads during playback and record operations to hold the tape against the heads. Pressure
pads are bits of felt on spring-loaded arms. With much use, the
felt may become caked and glazed with dirt. When this happens,
the pads may press the tape unevenly against the heads causing
irregular head wear with consequent tone and volume distortion.
When the pads begin to get dirty, they may be cleaned with a
toothpick. By scraping the point of the toothpick over the pad,
the dirt will be loosened and the nap of the felt can be raised
again. If the pads are still too caked to use or are worn, they
should be replaced. Pad replacements are inexpensive and easy
to install: Cut the pad to size and affix it with cement. However, care should be taken to keep the cement off the surface of
the pad which touches the head.

Tape Quality

The quality of tape used will also determine to a large extent how long the heads will last. Good tape will be smoother
(cutting down wear) and cleaner (leaving less oxide behind) than
most inexpensive off-brand tape. Pointers on tape buying are
given in Chapter 4.

Head Alignment

Head alignment refers to the position of the heads in relation
to the recording tape. Ideally, the head gap should be able to
touch the tape when the gap length is precisely at right angles
to the edge of the tape, perfectly parallel to the side of the
tape, and exactly centered on the proper track location. This
sentence refers to the five attitude adjustments for head alignment: touching the tape = tangency and contact; at right angles
to the tape edge = azimuth; parallel to the tape sides = tilt;
and centered on track location = height. Since alignment problems typically affect only the azimuth, the one adjustment screw
found at the base of recorder heads changes the azimuth attitude.

Misalignment can result from ordinary use, uneven head wear,
and shock. It will affect recording in the following ways: A
misaligned erase head is not so important provided the head

covers the entire track width. Severe problems may occur, however, when trying to play tapes made on someone else's recorder,
when recording tapes to be played on other recorders, or when
separate record and playback heads on the same machine are out
of alignment with respect to each other. In these cases, there
may be a drastic loss in high pitches on playback.

If recorder-to-recorder compatibility is important or if you
suspect that the separate record and playback heads on your recorder are not in parallel position, you should have a technician
check the head alignment and make the necessary adjustments.
For this critical task, he will use special instruments and an
alignment tape containing tones at different pitches. This is
not a do-it-yourself job except as a last resort.

TIP: Problems with head alignment should be suspected only
when you get no improvement in quality after having thoroughly cleaned and demagnetized the heads, inspected pressure
and tension, and tried different grades of tape on the
machine.

For a single record/playback head, adjustment is not difficult. As the alignment tape is played, the head adjustment
screw should be turned slightly with a screwdriver to tilt the
head until all the tones are heard at their loudest volume. The
head is then aligned.

For separate playback and record heads, the playback head is
adjusted as above. The record head is then adjusted by recording the tone tape being played on another recorder (with correct
alignment) and monitoring what is recorded through the playback
head. The record head adjustment screw is turned until all the
tones are recorded at peak volume.

REPAIRS

When repairs must be made, there are several considerations
to bear in mind. First, if the recorder is still under warranty,
do not try to fix it yourself. Any tampering with the machine
may void the warranty. The recorder should be taken to the
closest authorized service center or packaged up and returned to
the manufacturer for repair.

If it is impractical or impossible to get authorized service
or if the recorder is beyond the warranty period, then take the
machine to a tape recorder specialist. In most cases, a tape
recorder specialist should be chosen over a television repairman
for service. The reasons are simple. First, the electronics
of the recorder are different from those of a television. Second, televisions do not have a set of mechanical features

comparable to the recorder transport system. Since mechanical
problems, more than electrical difficulties, force recorder
owners to seek help, it is important that the repairman know
this aspect of the recorder thoroughly. Furthermore, it is
highly unlikely that a television serviceman would have the proper mechanical parts available. Third, from the standpoint of
repair time and per-hour cost, the recorder specialist is ordinarily to be preferred over the television repairman. He should
be able to diagnose problems and apply appropriate remedies more
quickly. Also, because of the vast number of manufacturers,
many overseas, and the rapid outdating of recorder models, there
are many occasions when parts are unavailable. In such cases,
the specialist is generally best qualified to make the needed
part.

Of course, if specialized help is not available, the best
help at hand should be taken. For the repairman whose specialty
is not tape recorders, the recorder service manual and parts inventory may be especially helpful. If you must tend to repairs
yourself, there are some general trouble-shooting guides available to help you. In this situation, it would help to have the
recorder service manual and a set of tools and extra parts
likely to be needed. This is especially important for those
traveling abroad. A list of tools and supplies necessary for
the general upkeep of your recorder is provided in Appendix 7.
For those going abroad, it would be a prudent move to visit a
reputable recorder technician to have him show you how the
mechanical system works and which parts you may need to have on
hand.

3 Microphone Selection and Care

In microphone shopping, as in recorder shopping, there is a wide variety of sizes, shapes, styles, and prices of equipment. If the right microphone is selected, not only will it serve you well, but it will also take only a minimum of special care.

MICROPHONE SELECTION

If a microphone comes with the recorder you select, it may be appropriate to wonder why we bother to discuss microphones. There are several important reasons why such a discussion is necessary. First, microphones do not come as standard equipment with all recorders. Rather than supply a microphone with quality inferior to that of the machine itself, some manufacturers do not include microphones with their higher quality tape recorders. This arrangement allows the buyer to select the particular type and quality of mike he wishes to use. Second, many mikes are of much lower quality than the recorders with which they are supplied. Since the recorder cannot produce anything better than what is fed into it, the buyer cannot get maximum performance from his recorder if he uses a poor microphone. Third, some of the microphones which come with lower priced recorders may not be suited to the climatic conditions of field work. Consequently, persons going abroad may want to buy a replacement microphone, rather than risk being without a mike if the original fails. Finally, certain recording purposes--for example, recording at a distance from the recorder, or at a distance from the sound source, or recording in the midst of noise--may not be adequately served with a standard equipment mike.

If, for any of the reasons above, you find yourself in a position of needing to select a microphone, this chapter should aid you in choosing the right one. As with tape recorders, there is no single microphone that is right for all purposes. For this reason, the questions we raise ask you to consider your particular circumstances--what kind of recording you intend to do and what kind of recorder you will use. The discussion with each question will help you determine the specific microphone characteristics most suitable for your recording demands.

Where Are the Sounds that Are to Be Recorded?

Every microphone has a certain direction or directions from which it best receives sound waves. The question above asks you to visualize where the sound source is likely to be in relation to the microphone you use. The way you answer this question should have a direct bearing on your decision about the directionality (or direction of pickup) of the microphone you choose. In general, if you answer the question in more than one way, it may take more than one microphone to meet your needs.

In order to discuss this question and provide criteria upon which to make a wise decision, the different types of directionality are discussed. Then we turn to the interaction between directionality, sound source, and microphone location.

Direction of Pickup. There are four basic pickup patterns available among microphones.

1. Omnidirectional. The most common pickup pattern is omnidirectional (also called nondirectional). Of the pickup elements to be discussed below, the carbon, ceramic, crystal, dynamic, and condenser mikes are essentially omnidirectional, although their directionality can be modified. An omnidirectional mike is nominally sensitive to sound coming from all sides. The fact is, however, that it is not equally responsive to sound from all 360 degrees in the surrounding three-dimensional space. It is equally receptive to only about 300 degrees of that space. The question of how a microphone buyer knows which portions of the circle are highly or weakly sensitive is discussed at the end of this section.

2. Bidirectional. The bidirectional mike (also called the figure eight) *hears* from two directions, the front and back; it is relatively insensitive on the two sides. Only the ribbon mike discussed below is inherently bidirectional, although it can be altered to provide unidirectional pickup. To visualize the shape of the reception area, it is helpful to think of two cones extending out from two opposite faces of the mike.

3. Unidirectional. A mike with unidirectional pickup is most sensitive to the sounds entering from straight ahead; it is less sensitive to those entering from the sides and almost *deaf* to those from behind. Because of this selective pattern, the unidirectional mike can be used to focus on sound in the midst of noise, and, if associated with a public address system, can effectively control feedback howl.

The term *cardioid,* a synonym for unidirectional, provides a more graphic description of the pattern. It brings to mind a three-dimensional Valentine's Day heart. The mike can be thought of as being in the depression of the heart, directed toward the point. If the unidirectional mike is placed face up and low with respect to the surrounding sound sources, it can serve as a kind of omnidirectional mike.

A cardioid mike has a reception angle of about 180 degrees, but its directional discrimination differs with the frequencies it is picking up. It is most directional for high frequency sounds which travel in a rather straight line, and least directional for low frequencies which are able to maneuver around curves. Thus, the tendency of the mike is to pick up treble sounds best if they are directly in front and center of the cardioid pattern. Bass sounds, however, can be picked up even from slightly behind the microphone, in the rounded areas of the heart-shaped pattern.

The relatively greater proportion of bass response received by cardioid microphones gives rise to what is called the *proximity effect*--an exaggeration of the bass frequencies (up to about 500 Hz). The proximity effect shows up when the sound source is within two feet of the microphone. While this effect colors the sound, it is not necessarily a negative feature. For voice recording, it can make a thin voice sound fuller, and any voice somewhat more mellow. For music recorded within the two-foot range, however, such an overemphasis of the bass response is definitely undesirable.

4. Hyperdirectional. Special housing designs and conditions of use make it possible to narrow the angle of sound reception. The appearance of a long, thin microphone housing--a tube of eighteen inches up to several feet--has generated a number of descriptive terms: long throw, cannon, gun. This design provides a more selective pickup than the cardioid design. A sound must be precisely within the narrow reception cone in order to be received by the mike. Sounds at 25, 50, 100, or 300 feet can be picked up outdoors with reasonable clarity. The better the pickup and the more directional it is, the higher the microphone price.

A slightly different and earlier version of the long-throw mike is known as the rifle, shotgun, or multi-tube directional microphone. These names depict a set of tubes of different lengths bundled together and flush at one end. A generating element, placed close to the flush end, transmits sound from the tubes to an amplifier and on to an earphone or recorder.

The different tube lengths serve two purposes. One is to resonate like the pipes of an organ to specific frequencies arriving on the axis of the tubes; the other is to put off-axis sounds out of phase so they are self-canceling. The result is a highly directional pickup pattern useful especially for outdoor recording of sounds at distances of up to 200 yards.[1] When recording at a distance from the sound source, another method of achieving hyperdirectional pickup is by the use of a parabolic reflector. This device is discussed under accessories at the end of this chapter.

When recording close to the sound source but in a very noisy environment, a hyperdirectional pattern will improve quality. This pattern is available in a small, hand-held mike which has been so tailored that all sounds outside the center line of reception (the axis) are canceled, and only sounds on the axis are turned into electrical energy. The name appropriately labeling this microphone is *noise canceling*. It is used with the recordist's face touching or nearly touching the housing.

When shopping for a microphone, how can the buyer tell which pickup pattern a microphone has and, more specifically, precisely which directions in the pattern are the most and least sensitive to sound? The directionality of a microphone is identified either on the mike itself or on the specification sheet by one of the directional terms used above. Furthermore, if it is a good quality microphone, certain specifications included with the instrument can be of considerable help in determining the details of the pattern and how to position the mike when recording.

In microphone testing, technicians prepare what is called a *polar response graph* or *polar plot*, which shows how sensitive the microphone is to particular frequencies on all of its sides. It takes no sophistication in electronics or acoustic matters to interpret or benefit from the information on the graph. If the microphone is truly omnidirectional, the lines drawn for each test tone would form a complete, smooth circle equidistant around the center. If the mike is not omnidirectional either for all tones or on all sides for one tone, the line will dip toward the center of the graph indicating less sensitivity. Other mikes are tested in the same way. The value of the polar plot is that

it will tell the microphone user how his microphone should be
placed in order to keep his subjects within the optimum contours of the polar plot.

Directionality, Sound Source, and Microphone Placement. A
knowledgeable decision about microphone directionality must take
into account the characteristics of the sound source and the position and distance of the mike in relation to that sound source.
The characteristics of the sound source most relevant to the
directionality of a microphone are (1) how spread out the sound
source is, and (2) how much competition there is from ambient
noises. Microphone position and distance relative to the sound
source have a direct bearing on the pickup pattern because the
mike must be sensitive to (3) the direction(s) from which the
sound arrives at the mike, and (4) the distance the sound must
travel to reach the mike.

These four features are interdependent in their effect on the
sound entering the microphone. The approach we take in our discussion of directionality is to ask you to consider these four
features in your situation. While not all recording circumstances can be anticipated, some reflection on the character of
your work may help you project the likely conditions under which
you will be using a microphone.

First of all, what do the four distinctions mean in terms of
actual recording situations? Try to answer each question below
for yourself in light of your circumstances. Your answers will
lead you to discover the pickup pattern(s) best suited to your
needs.

1. How spread out is the sound source? The angle formed by
imaginary lines from the mike to the two sides of a sound source
may be narrow or wide. In the case of a single speaker or a
single player of some musical instrument, the mike-source angle
is narrow. A panel discussion or an orchestra forms a wide mike-
source angle. The issue in the matter of microphone directionality is whether the reception angle of the microphone is *wide
enough* to include all sounds emanating from the source.

2. How much competition is there from ambient noises? If
the recordist can pick his time and place of recording, he has
the possibility of capturing target sounds with little interference from outside noises. However, with the exception of
staged settings, we ordinarily encounter our target sounds in
the company of undesirable noise--transportation sounds, foot-
steps, echos, and so forth. In such cases, the microphone pickup
pattern most preferred would be the one which would allow the
recordist to focus on the wanted sounds and to put the unwanted
sounds in the deaf portion of the pattern. The aim, then, is to
use a pattern which is *not too wide* for the sound source.

3. From which direction does the sound arrive at the microphone? The target sound may arrive at the microphone from only one general direction, or it may arrive from all sides of the microphone simultaneously. In the case of a narrow-angle sound source, two speakers opposite each other with a mike between them present a situation different from one person talking into a microphone. A wide-angle sound coming potentially from all sides, such as that coming from a group of children at play or from speaker-audience interaction, will envelop the microphone. The reception angle needed for situations like these is different from what is required for either narrow-angle sound sources or wide-angle sound coming from only one direction, as when several speakers are on one side of a table, or when a choir sings. The question for microphone directionality is whether one or both sides of the mike should be receptive to sound.

4. Will the microphone be close to or far from the sound source? The terms *close to* and *far from* are to be understood as relative to the sound source being recorded. For example, in relation to a widely spread out sound source, *close* will be less than about ten feet, while *far* will mean more than ten feet. In relation to a sound source covering a narrow angle, *close* will mean less than about three feet, and *far*, more than three feet. The distance from mike to source will have a bearing on how wide the mike reception cone should be.

Having discussed the variability within each factor, let us look at how these factors can combine and what the implications are for selecting microphone directionality. Figure 9 presents all the possibilities, from the most ideal situation across the top of the chart to the least ideal across the bottom of the chart. The quality of recording possible in the poorest of circumstances will not be the same as that possible when recording in the best of circumstances. Microphone directionality cannot eliminate the effect of less than ideal circumstances; it can only reduce the effect somewhat, depending on how poor the circumstances are. Nevertheless, suggestions are given about directionality for all situations with an appreciation for the fact that at times there is no alternative available but to record under inferior conditions.

When reading Figure 9, start on the left. At each pair of arrows, make a choice according to what you project your situation to be. At the far right you will find suggestions for microphone directionality, abbreviated Uni, Omni, Bi, and Hyper.

Sound Relative to Microphone Position   Microphone
Directionality

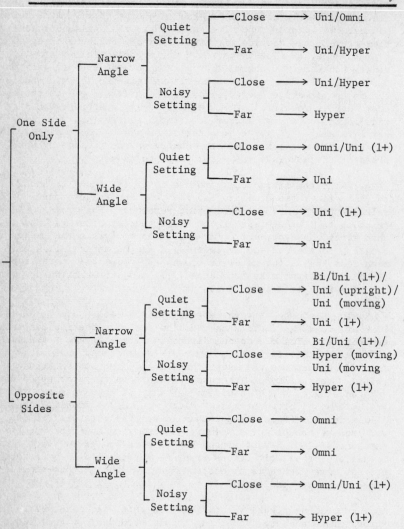

Fig. 9. Factors Affecting the Choice of Microphone Directionality

Certain situations may be handled in more than one way; the options are separated by slashes. If possible, experimentation with the options is recommended. When a single individual is recording (one side, narrow angle) the best reception will be achieved by using a unidirectional mike on a lavalier about the speaker's neck. Where more than one (1+) microphone is suggested, they may be merged into one line by a mixer or go separately to different channels. To pick up a wide angle sound on one side of the mike, more than one unidirectional mike may be used. For example, a highly successful setup is to use two unidirectional mikes with pickup ends seven to eight inches apart so that the mikes make an angle of 110 degrees. Placed in the center and above a group, the complementary cardioid patterns will give commendable results.

The notation *moving* following certain microphones is to indicate that the particular microphone is usable if the sound can be captured by moving the mike by hand. *Upright* refers to a unidirectional mike placed face up and low in relation to the sound source. Hyperdirectional is found with *close* and *far* microphone positions. When it occurs after *close*, the hyperdirectional mike is the noise-canceling variety; when it occurs after *far*, it is the long-throw or shotgun variety, or even the parabolic reflector system.

> TIP: As Figure 9 indicates, the great majority of all situations can be adequately handled by one or more unidirectional microphones. About a third of the situations can use an omnidirectional mike. Bi- and hyperdirectional mikes have limited use but serve largely where no other microphone can perform as well.

What Quality of Sound Do I Need?

The above question was also asked in our discussion of tape recorder selection. The assumption here is that if you have purchased a recorder to give you a certain quality of sound reproduction, you will also be interested in utilizing that quality to full measure when you record. The only thing preventing full use of the recorder's capability is the capacity of the microphone you use. The question about sound quality, then, must be answered with two factors in mind: (1) the kind of target sound to be recorded, and (2) the quality of reproduction the recorder is capable of.

Target Sound to Be Recorded. First of all, the target sound partly defines the *frequency response* and the *smoothness* of the response needed from a microphone. If the target sound is to be exclusively speech, one set of requirements is appropriate; if the sound is to include music as well, another set of requirements is necessary.

1. Frequency Response. The frequency response of a microphone is the range of sound pitches it is capable of translating
into electrical energy. For speech, the sound pitches, measured
in cycles per second (Hz) are approximately 100 Hz-9,000 Hz for
a male speaker and about 250 Hz-10,000 Hz for a female speaker.[2]

It is not necessary, of course, to have a 10,000 Hz recording
capability to be able to understand the speech recorded. The
telephone is a good example of this fact. The mouthpiece of the
handset is a microphone with a frequency range of 200 Hz-
3,400 Hz.[3] Although some people take it as a mild insult that
others do not consistently recognize them by their voices over
the telephone, it is not necessarily the fault of the listener.
The telephone band width was not established for the purpose of
conveying speaker uniqueness, but rather speaker intelligibility.

In recording, the issue is not so much, Is the speech intelligible? It is often rather, Is the particular speaker identifi-
able and also natural sounding? A microphone frequency response
up to 10,000 Hz will capture all the unique components of a person's voice; a response of 8,000 Hz will do almost as well.
Thus, if speech is to be the major recording content, the microphone used should have a frequency response of about 100 Hz-
8,000 Hz for good voice reproduction or about 50 Hz-10,000 Hz
for excellent reproduction.

Music makes more stringent demands on equipment quality than
does speech. Both ends of the frequency response must be extended. The low note on an organ is about 16 Hz; the high pitch
produced by a snare drum is around 15,000 Hz.[4] Overtones and
instrument operation noises require an even wider span of pitches
than suggested by the organ or drum. As a guideline, the range
of 30 Hz-15,000 Hz is the minimum range recognized for high fidelity sound. This means that a response of 50 Hz-10,000 Hz,
superb for voice, is useful for only less critically judged music. Thus, a microphone for music should approach at least the
high fidelity minimum.

2. Smoothness. The feature of smoothness is as important as
frequency response. Smoothness refers to how uniformly the frequency range can be reproduced by a particular microphone. Are
certain portions of the reproduction range, say the bass, louder
than other portions; or is the treble section of the range exaggerated?

Ideally, in microphone testing, all frequencies within the
capability of the microphone should be reproduced at the same
loudness. If a graph were drawn with the band of frequencies
along the bottom and the units of volume up the left side, the
ideal response would be a flat line from one side of the graph
to the other, indicating no deviation from perfect reproduction.

Ideal smoothness is not achieved by any microphone. Certain frequencies in the range are reproduced with greater or lesser loudness than all the rest. Technicians measure degrees of loudness in units called decibels (db). A one- to two-decibel difference in volume is as small a difference as the human ear can detect. When microphones are tested, technicians determine the smoothness of a microphone frequency response in terms of how many decibels each frequency varies above or below a per-fectly flat response. They map out their test results for each microphone on a frequency response graph as described above. The graph is easy to read; so when you buy a microphone, examine the graph for two things—the frequency range and the decibel variation. If the response varies no more than ±2 db, it is ex-cellent and is considered essentially flat. Lesser quality is reflected as the decibel variation increases. The maximum ac-ceptable response deviation should be no more than ±5 db or ±6 db. If no frequency response graph accompanies the mike, but specifications give frequency range and smoothness figures, pay attention to the specifications. If no smoothness figures are provided, be suspicious of the quality. If the microphone is to be used as a part of a public address system, the greater the peaks and valleys across the frequency response, the greater the feedback or howl problems will be.

Reproduction Capability of the Recorder. The second factor to consider when judging the reproduction quality of a micro-phone is the equipment with which it is to be used. The target sound alone should not determine the quality of reproduction chosen for a mike. The quality of your recorder should always be kept in mind. If you are buying a replacement mike in order to get one which will allow you to make use of as much of the frequency response of your recorder as possible, you will be happily surprised. The quality of your new recordings will make it appear that you had bought a new tape recorder instead. But you will be disappointed if you purchase a mike with a frequency range wider than your recorder is able to reproduce.

TIP: While the mike limits what the recorder can record, the recorder limits what it can accept from the mike. Efficiency suggests that both mike and recorder have frequency ranges as similar as possible. Economy suggests that the frequency response of your mike be no wider than is needed for the re-cording purposes you have in mind.

Will My Recorder Accept Any Microphone?

Up to this point we have discussed three microphone features, directionality, frequency response, and smoothness. In order to answer the question above, we will be led to consider three more microphone characteristics: pickup element, sensitivity, and impedance.

Essentially the question of microphone-recorder compatibility revolves around electricity. A tape recorder operates by means of some form of electricity. Its ability to accept a microphone depends on the nature of the electricity the microphone produces and sends to the recorder to use. The concerns of this section, then, are (1) how the microphone translates sound into electricity (pickup element), (2) how strong the electricity is that reaches the recorder (sensitivity), and (3) whether the recorder is sensitive to the electricity produced (impedance).

These concerns should be important to everyone planning to buy a microphone; to ignore them is to court grief. A mismatched mike and recorder can be as bad as no microphone or recorder at all. The fact that electricity is the main topic of this section should not frighten the reader away. All crucial aspects of mike-recorder compatibility can be explained easily, nontechnically, yet thoroughly enough to guide the microphone buyer in evaluating any piece of equipment accurately.

Pickup Element. A microphone is a device which takes one form of energy--sound--and converts it into another form of energy--electricity. This conversion is brought about by the pickup element inside the microphone. There are many kinds of pickup elements, each with its own strengths and weaknesses. Only the most common pickup elements will be discussed and evaluated in this section. While the central question is whether your recorder will accept a microphone with a particular element, an equally important question is whether *you* will accept it. The discussion below will help you answer both questions.

1. Carbon Microphone. We begin the analysis with the most common of all microphones. Our comments are brief, however, because the carbon microphone has little to offer the serious language recordist.

Commercially, carbon microphones are used primarily with communications equipment for voice transmission. Carbon mikes are found with aviation and nautical communication sets, car-to-base radios as in police cars, taxicabs, delivery trucks, and so forth. Our most intimate contact with the carbon mike, however, is in our use of the telephone. The mouthpiece contains such a mike.

What makes communications equipment different from tape recording is primarily the circumstances of mike use. First, the mobile communication setting is filled with noise. The microphone needed is one with poor sensitivity. The user must then speak loudly enough to get above the noise. Second, noise renders high frequencies useless, so the microphone used need not respond to such frequencies. Third, since speech intelligibility

is all that is required, only the low and middle frequencies are
of value. The carbon mike can accommodate these circumstances
easily and inexpensively with its low sensitivity and narrow
frequency range (from about 100 Hz up to about 4,000 Hz).

The very features which make the carbon element fine for communications situations make it unfit for tape recording. A tape
recorder would have to be specially designed to accept the low
sensitivity of the carbon mike. Furthermore, language recordists
have higher goals for their voice recordings than mere intelligibility, yet the frequency response of a carbon mike simply
cannot reproduce sound much beyond what is needed for basic intelligibility.

2. Crystal and Ceramic Microphones. Crystal and ceramic
pickup elements are called piezoelectrics (from the Greek *piezien*
meaning *to bend*), because the sound forces the element out of
shape, thereby creating electricity. Piezoelectric elements
make the least expensive microphones. Such microphones are commonly supplied with lower priced recorders.

The crystal microphone is so called because it is made from a
naturally occurring salt crystal. One of the problems with the
crystal is that it is easily damaged by heat, humidity, and
shock. The crystal has a natural level of moisture which should
not be altered. In dry climates, however, the moisture in the
crystal will dry up; in humid climates, the crystal will absorb
moisture and dissolve. To counter these effects, some manufacturers seal the crystal element in some waterproof material.
But, if the microphone is dropped, the fragile element is still
likely to break. Any one of these conditions will render the
microphone useless.

The ceramic microphone gets its name from the fact that it
uses a small piece of china for a pickup element. It is essentially a man-made crystal. As compared with the crystal element,
however, the ceramic is more rugged. It is not affected by temperature extremes nor by humidity and is not quite so fragile.

Both ceramic and crystal microphones have approximately the
same electrical characteristics. While both can boast a rather
high sensitivity, neither of them can reproduce a wide range of
frequencies nor reproduce even a narrow range smoothly. Most
piezoelectric elements can transmit frequencies no higher than
about 7,000 Hz. Using a very carefully made ceramic element,
the highest frequency possible is about 10,000 Hz. However,
even within this range, the response is not smooth; piezoelectrics tend to reproduce the high and low frequencies very weakly
and the middle frequencies strongly.

TIP: Not infrequently, the reason many recordists replace
their microphones is because the microphone included with
their original equipment used a ceramic or crystal pickup
element. For reasons of poor frequency response, suscepti-
bility to damage by climate and hard use, and limited distance the mike may be used from the recorder (see impedance
discussion below), recordists select other pickup elements
for their needs.

3. Dynamic Microphone. The dynamic microphone (also called
the moving coil microphone) is appropriately referred to as the
workhorse of the recording industry. Its characteristics as
well as its price reveal why this is so. It is justifiably considered by many as the best compromise between quality and price.

The dynamic pickup element is one of the most rugged elements
in use. It is not affected by temperature extremes or humidity.
If dropped, it is far less likely to be ruined than other elements. While its endurance is good, so is its performance. The
dynamic element is capable of smoothly reproducing the full range
of audio frequencies. Although it has basically an omnidirectional pickup pattern, changes in the housing design can give it
a unidirectional pickup with only a small loss in sensitivity.
As we shall see in our discussion of impedance, the dynamic element can also be used at great distances from the recorder, unlike the carbon or piezoelectric microphones.

It should be noted that a dynamic microphone is not necessarily good because it is of the dynamic type; there is wide variety in price and quality among these microphones. Dynamic
mikes are often provided as original equipment with medium to
higher priced recorders. This is no indication that the microphone is equal in quality to the recorder; typically, it is not.

TIP: The language recordist would do well to look seriously
at this type of microphone especially if rough service and/or
adverse climatic conditions are in store for the mike. The
dynamic pickup element takes little care, yet provides superb
voice and music reproduction according to the quality of the
instrument.

4. Condenser Microphone. The condenser microphone (also
known as the capacitor microphone) was once exclusively a professional's mike because of price and quality. Advancements in
microphone research, however, have now put the price in the
moderate to low range and the quality wherever the recordist
wants it.

The condenser microphone at its best can reproduce the entire
audio range (20 Hz-20,000 Hz) with almost perfect smoothness.

Furthermore, the buyer has a choice of either a unidirectional
or omnidirectional pickup pattern. Because of developments in
this microphone, it is nearly on a par with the dynamic microphone for ruggedness and reliability.

By itself, this potentially superb piece of equipment gener-
ates the weakest signal of any microphone. By itself, it could
not be used with any recorder. In order to magnify the signal
so that the recorder can use it, the condenser mike must be
linked to an externally-powered amplifier (called a preamplifier
or preamp) all its own. With this amplifier, any desired level
of output is available.

Two advancements are responsible for bringing the condenser
mike out of its exclusively professional domain. The first is
the use of a permanently charged material (electret) in the
generating element rather than externally charged material. The
second development was in the use of transistorized battery-
operated amplifiers small enough to fit inside the mike cylinder
itself. With these two developments, bulk and expensive price
were overcome at the same time.

Electret condenser mikes can be designed for any level of
quality, and they run the gamut. At one extreme, by exploiting
to the full their high reliability, excellent frequency response,
and low distortion capabilities, electret condensers compete in
the most demanding of professional circles. At the other extreme, we find electret condenser mikes built into the most inexpensive cassette recorders.

One storage precaution must be exercised for the electret condenser mike: The electret can lose its charge if subjected to
the combination of high temperatures (120° F or above) and high
humidity. For example, storage in the trunk of a car in hot,
humid weather could damage the electret irreparably.

TIP: The electret condenser microphone merits careful consideration as an original or a replacement mike. Since the
mike has potentially excellent characteristics, the recordist
can certainly find the quality he wants in an equally attractive price bracket.

5. Ribbon Microphone. Another high quality microphone, once
popular in the broadcasting industry because of its wide frequency range and its ideally smooth response, is the ribbon microphone, known also as the velocity mike. Sound entering the
microphone strikes a thin strip of aluminum foil and sets it
vibrating, creating electrical energy.

The ribbon mike might have much to offer the language recordist were it not for certain very serious problems. The most

important problem is that the foil ribbon used in many microphones is ultrafragile. It must be handled with painstaking
care because wind or even sudden movement can ruin the pickup
element. Obviously, this microphone could not be used in outdoor recording. This problem is being overcome; some elements
are   now as durable as dynamic elements. A second problem is
that the mike requires fine mechanical adjustments in order to
work properly--an inconvenience even for indoor recording.
Third, although the microphone housing can be altered, this
pickup element has essentially a bidirectional pickup pattern.
Nearly all bidirectional microphones use the ribbon element. As
Figure 9 discussed earlier in this chapter indicates, the bidirectional pattern serves well in only a few situations.
Fourth, ribbon microphones are very expensive.

   Sensitivity. Sound is the input to a microphone pickup element; electricity is the output of the element. Sensitivity is
a description of the input-output relationship. Since both the
quantity of sound reaching the mike and the quantity of electricity leaving the mike can be measured, technicians can describe how much electricity the mike can produce for a given
amount of sound. A mike is said to be more sensitive the greater
the electrical output and less sensitive the smaller the electrical output.

   The question of whether a particular mike will be acceptable
to your recorder, unfortunately, can be answered satisfactorily
only by a trial and error procedure. It is not possible simply
to look at the specification sheets of a mike and recorder and
tell whether the two pieces of equipment will be compatible.
The reason for this is that there are at least a half-dozen different and mathematically unrelated ways being used to measure
the input-output relationship. Consequently, microphone specifications differ from manufacturer to manufacturer, and recorders
rarely specify the range of sensitivities they can accept.

   The best way to check on compatibility is to use the mike
with the recorder. If, on the one hand, you can produce satisfactory recording results with no increase in the normal record
level setting, the mike is within the acceptable sensitivity
range of the recorder. If, on the other hand, you must record
at a much higher record level setting than before in order to
get a good recording, the mike is probably not sensitive enough
for your recorder. By using the mike with full input volume,
you will add much background hiss to the tape. Another microphone with greater sensitivity will probably solve the problem.

   TIP: The sensitivity issue is not as clearcut as the microphone shopper might like. Different rating methods are in
   current use; information about sensitivity in recorder specifications is lacking; most good microphones seem to have

sensitivities in approximately the same range. The advice
at this point might be simply to ignore sensitivity alto-
gether. However, an awareness of this issue is felt to be
helpful to a microphone buyer so that he will recognize sensitivity as a potential problem in mike-recorder compatibility and as a factor which should be checked by a test
procedure when testing other aspects of a mike.

Impedance. Impedance is a characteristic of an electrical
system which tells how responsive it is to the electricity passing through the system. The unit used to measure impedance (or
the resistance to the flow of electricity) is the ohm, symbolized
as Ω or Z.

A high impedance system--recorder or microphone--is not in
itself better than a low impedance system, or vice versa. There
is, however, one significant reason for preferring a low impedance microphone over a high impedance one: the distance the
microphone can be used from the recorder.

There are many occasions when it is either inconvenient, in
poor taste, or impractical to have the recorder with the microphone when recording. If the recordist is moving among people,
his movement is facilitated if he is carrying only his mike. If
he is recording in some formal setting, such as a wedding or a
musical production, he will want his equipment to be as unobtrusive as possible. The microphone may be in view, but the recorder should be out of sight. If the recordist is making a
covert recording on-location, a long cable from mike to concealed recording equipment may be a necessity. If he needs to
have at least one hand free, or if his recorder is simply too
heavy to carry easily under one arm, he may prefer to leave the
recorder in one place. These are just a few of the reasons some
recordists find long mike lines a convenience.

Unfortunately, a high impedance mike cannot be used very far
from the recorder (over fifteen feet). With longer lines, high
frequencies are lost and a hum appears in the recording as the
lines pick up stray electrical impulses in the vicinity (from
the ground or from other electrical equipment). For this reason
many recordists prefer low impedance microphones which may be
used at great distances--hundreds of feet--from the recorder
without sacrificing reproduction quality.

Even though a high impedance (above 10,000 Z) or a low impedance (below 600 Z) microphone may be chosen for recording,
the two kinds of mikes may not be indiscriminately plugged into
any tape recorder. While it will not damage the mike or the recorder to be mismatched, the recording results will be inferior

if a high impedance mike is used with a low impedance recorder.
The sound reproduced will be distorted, full of hum, or not
present at all on the tape.

The problem of mismatched impedances can easily be eliminated.
First, specifications for good microphones indicate clearly
whether the system is high or low impedance and specifically
what the high and low ratings are. Recorder specifications are
also helpful. They will give information about the impedances
the recorder input jack will accept.

Second, many of the better microphones are dual impedance.
Although the pickup element is inherently either high or low impedance, many mikes incorporate a transformer so that by a simple
rewiring operation, a reversal of a plug, or a flip of a switch,
a high impedance microphone can be converted to a low impedance
mike.

Third, if you want to record at a distance from your high impedance recorder with a low impedance microphone, your low impedance mike can be plugged into an impedance matching transformer located near your recorder. A transformer is a relatively
inexpensive device. Some higher priced recorders come equipped
with transformers built into the input jacks; others have input
transformers available as options.

TIP: As a general rule, a microphone can be plugged into
any input having an impedance equal to or greater than that
of the mike. Thus, a low impedance mike is usable almost
anywhere. The only safe way to be sure there is no change
in sound characteristics is to try out the mike and recorder
together. Check the recording carefully for evidence of
distortion, hum, weak volume.

Which Microphone Accessories Should Be Considered?

Accessories vary widely in importance; some are essential
while others are of marginal value. The discussion in this
section is designed to improve your evaluation of commonly
available options. These options fall into categories related
to the stages in getting sound to the recorder.

To Record or Not to Record. We can put a recorder into record mode but still not record if we have an auxiliary means to
control recorder operation. Two such means associated with microphones are available. One is manual; the other, automatic.
Both are usable only on recorders equipped for them.

An on/off switch is the manual way of regulating whether the
reels turn after pressing the record buttons. As mentioned in

Chapter 1, this electrical pause is often built into the microphone housing and is essentially a circuit breaker. We refer
the reader to Chapter 1 for a discussion of the merits of the
accessory and how to have a switch without buying one in a mike.

The automatic operation control is commonly called a *voice-
activated microphone*. It governs recorder operation according
to the level of incoming sound. When the input volume is sufficiently strong, the microphone starts the record process.
When the volume trails off, or when there is silence, the mike
will cause the recorder to pause.

The claim for the voice-activated microphone is that it will
take care of the recorder during conferences, dictation, and so
forth, recording only when there is something to record and
thereby conserving tape. While such a claim is true in general,
there are certain characteristics of this feature that should be
noted. First, it is for voice only, not music. Second, it is
for voice recording in which quality is not important. When the
machine is activated, the first few syllables of input will pass
without being recorded. If recording begins before the tape has
reached its maximum speed, the sound being captured will be distorted. As long as the input volume is sufficiently high, recording will proceed. But as soon as it drops below the critical
level, the microphone will de-activate the recorder, despite the
possible importance of what is being said. It is easy to see
that the quality of voice recording will not be high. Under-
standably, too, the loss of initial material and the cut-off
during soft portions will render this feature unusable for music
recording.

From Sound to Mike. Certain accessories optimize recording
at different distances from the sound source and under varying
conditions.

Windscreens help prevent the roar of wind noise in an outdoor
recording. They also reduce pops and hiss encountered with certain consonants when recording close to the mike. Windscreens
are not offered as optional equipment with all mikes. However,
many windscreens are flexible enough to fit over the reception
end of most slender microphone cylinders. Windscreen material
of either foam rubber or plastic foam can be purchased for
custom-made windscreens. One to three layers of silk on the
microphone face will also serve as an adequate windscreen.[5]

There are a number of devices available to hold the mike at
desired distances and positions. Any lightweight microphone can
be attached to a lavalier and placed around the speaker's neck.
A cord fastened to a microphone by a rubber band will serve
nicely. Some mikes are small enough to be worn on a pin or tie

clip. These holding devices provide a constant, ideally close mike-mouth recording distance.

While good input volume can be assured, the closeness of the mike to the mouth tends to emphasize the bass tones. This is the *proximity effect* mentioned earlier in the chapter. It is generally not objectionable, although in professional circles mikes used at such distances are especially designed to equalize for this effect.

Microphone stands can put a mike at close to intermediate distances from the sound source. If a desk or floor stand is purchased, it should be heavy and tip-proof. Available for good microphones are threaded socket attachments usable with any standard mike stand. The standard socket size is 5/8-inch diameter, 27 threads per inch. Adjustable booms can be fixed to mike stands to extend a mike above the sound source.

Mike stands and booms, however, need not be purchased; homemade holders using common materials can serve as well as the manufactured models. For example, with a pair of scissors a simple stand can be cut from a block of household sponge. A trough is carved to hold the mike at precisely the best angle for use on a table.

When recording outdoors at a considerable distance from the sound source, a parabolic reflector in combination with an ordinary unidirectional mike is a useful accessory. The reflector is a concave dish which focuses sound at a single point in the front and center of the dish where a microphone is positioned facing the reflector. The larger the parabolic dish, the greater the mike-source distance can be. Among the largest reflectors were those built by the British before radar was invented as an air raid warning system. In order to pick up engine noises of hostile aircraft coming over the English Channel, forty-foot concrete dishes were built into the hillsides of England. Portable dishes, of course, are available ranging in size from eighteen inches to three feet and made of plastic, wood, or aluminum. They all operate on the same principle: sound concentrated at one point will appear to be magnified. A two-foot reflector, for example, can pick up voices clearly at seventy-five feet. In Figure 9, a parabolic reflector can be used for long-distance recording whenever a hyperdirectional pickup pattern is suggested.

From Mike to Recorder. Sound energy converted to electrical energy must make its way to the recorder. It will do so over mike cables. The most convenient cable is detachable from the mike. Even if this is not possible, cables of different lengths can be easily joined according to the recordist's needs. Better

microphones are often sold without plugs on the ends of the
cables. The recordist must choose the plug type appropriate for
his recorder.

As discussed earlier in this chapter, cable lengths of over
fifteen feet should be avoided when using a high impedance recorder. An accessory to eliminate this problem is the impedance
matching transformer. It is connected to the input of the recorder and allows the use of cables of any length.

Only low impedance mikes can be used with long cables. If
the recordist has a microphone with a dual impedance switch on
it, he can use his mike for either impedance as needed. The
switch is an additional feature which saves him the purchase of
a low impedance mike. Of course, when the recordist has a
choice, the best solution to these problems is to record with a
low impedance recorder only.

In some recording situations, several microphones can be used
to advantage. Unless the recorder has as many channels (inputs)
as there are mikes, a mixer will be required to merge multiple
inputs into a smaller number of output lines. Mixers differ in
their input-output capacities, but most will have an independent
volume-control knob for each input so that the best balance for
each channel is achieved.

A closing word about microphone selection should be a word
about the actual purchase. A good quality microphone represents
a considerable investment. The dealer should recognize this and
accord the buyer every privilege to insure his satisfaction with
the purchase. This is standard procedure among reputable deal-
ers. No matter how much a salesman may assure him of a perfect
match, the purchaser cannot be certain of satisfaction until he
tries out the mike with his own recorder. There are simply too
many facts about microphone-recorder compatibility that are not
accessible through the specification sheet. The buyer should
make some arrangement with the dealer--a deposit for borrowing
the mike, a money-back guarantee, an in-store mike test with his
recorder--so that he can test the microphone with his equipment
before finalizing the purchase.

An opportunity to try out the mike and recorder together is
indispensable. Getting a written guarantee or warranty may prove
equally important. Be sure to get a guarantee or warranty covering the microphone and understand clearly what it provides.

Finally, do not let the list price be the final deciding criterion in microphone selection. Microphone prices are flexible
and negotiable. It is common knowledge among professionals that
discounts up to forty percent are possible on most microphones.

Once you have found the mike you like, do some comparative
shopping.

In summary, we have looked at microphone pickup elements,
pickup patterns, frequency response, sensitivity, impedance, and
certain accessories. We have tried to relate them to concrete
recording conditions. With the language recordist in mind, we
have tried to narrow the range of possibilities by suggesting
either the dynamic or electret condenser element, with unidirectional or omnidirectional pickup pattern, a frequency response
commensurate with either speech or music recording purposes, a
sensitivity to match the recorder used, and a low impedance if
the mike is to be used over fifteen feet from the recorder. We
have also listed the principal microphone accessories for different recording needs.

MICROPHONE CARE

Precautions are mentioned here for dynamic and condenser microphones only. When caring for mikes with other kinds of pickup
elements, use precautions appropriate to their characteristics
as described above.

In continuous high humidity, the moisture itself will probably
not do as much to harm the mike as the fungal growth which moisture encourages. Because the mike does have soldered connections, it is vulnerable to damage by fungus and should be kept
in a dehumidifying container. Never store the mike in an airtight container without some humidity-absorbing material also
present. The moisture from condensation inside the container
could be worse for the mike than the humidity outside. The
addition of high temperatures to high humidity can reduce the
ability of electrets in condenser microphones to retain their
charge. This situation should be carefully avoided.

Even though a dynamic or condenser microphone can take a
great deal more punishment than other kinds of microphones, it
is less likely to get out of adjustment if carried and stored in
a dustproof, padded case.

4 Recording Tape Selection

As recorder buyers, we face the job of selecting a tape recorder or microphone only a few times in many years. But consider how much more often we must choose recording tape. When buying a tape recorder or mike, there is ordinarily an abundance of data to vouch for the qualities and characteristics of these products. But for recording tape, there is little information available to help us make the right choice. Is one tape essentially as good as another? Are the differences between the varieties of tape superficial differences or important differences?

When we compare a number of boxes of open-reel tape, we notice the obvious differences. Inside the boxes, we see reels of different sizes, shapes, and colors, and tape of various lengths and hues. On the outside of the boxes, we notice the variety of trade names and product descriptions. Each box carries such information as 1 1/2 mil or 1 mil, polyester, plastic, or PVC, lubricated, splice free, high output, low print, and so forth. Finally, the price tag is there, too, in equally wide variety.

When we turn to look at cassette tapes, their highly uniform external appearance may deceive us into thinking there are no differences. The size and shape of cassette magazines are standardized world-wide. But inside the plastic housing the variety is there--in running time: C-60, C-90, C-120; in oxides: low noise, extra dynamic, high potency, CrO_2, and so on; in housing construction and packaging; and in price, perhaps the most noticeable of all.

What is behind these differences? What does this variety mean? In general, it means that some recording tape will yield

good recordings on your recorder with its present adjustment,
while other tape will not. It means that some tape may actually
damage your recorder severely, while other tape will not. It
also means that some tape will deteriorate under certain conditions, while other tape will not.

If you know what it means, the description on the label can
tell you a lot about a tape. In this chapter we will look into
the meaning of some of the less obvious differences in tape and
offer certain TIPS which you may find valuable in picking the
right product. If you wish to be a *tape detective*, it is also
possible to evaluate a tape which has no label or no detailed
descriptive information. We will provide some pointers for the
tape detective who is looking at unlabeled or off-brand tape or
tape with insufficient specifications.

In this chapter we assume that you are looking here for information about open-reel *or* cassette tape. The two types of
tapes share many characteristics, and for this reason, are discussed together. However, comments specific to open-reel or
cassette tape will be highlighted in the text to guide you in
finding the information you need.

Someone has described recording tape as a strip of thin plastic covered with barn paint. Such a definition will adequately
describe only the poorest recording tape, but in essence it
gives a correct picture of all tape, open-reel and cassette. In
more sophisticated terms, the *strip of thin plastic* is called
the *backing* (base material), and the *barn paint* is known as the
coating. The quality of a tape lies in the endurance and performance of these two basic components. We will discuss each in
turn.

HOW WELL WILL TAPE BACKINGS HOLD UP AND PERFORM?

An evaluation of base materials should include an examination
of the following features: For *endurance*, we look at (1) strength
and (2) weather and age resistance; for *performance*, we look at
(3) smoothness and (4) flexibility.

The *strength* of a backing gives us an idea of how much punishment the tape can take. A weak tape may break or stretch easily.
A strong backing can take more rough handling without breaking
or stretching. The strength of the backing determines how thin
the tape may be and thus how much tape may be wound onto a reel.

Common thicknesses of open-reel tape are 1 1/2 mil, 1 mil, and
1/2 mil. (One mil is one one-thousandth of an inch.) The table
in Appendix 2 specifies how much tape (in feet and meters) and
recording time (in hours and minutes) will be available on reels
of different sizes containing tape of different thicknesses.

Cassette tape uses thicknesses which run from about 1/2 mil to thinner than 1/4 mil. Computations of recording time, however, are far simpler than for open-reel tape because all cassette reels are the same size and recording time is used in the labeling system. Cassettes are labeled by letter and number, e.g., C-60, C-120. The prefixed letter refers to cassette; the digits refer to the number of minutes of recording time available when recorded on two passes *only*, as when using a two-track monophonic cassette machine. C-60 means 30 minutes on each of the two passes. Of course, if a C-60 cartridge is used on a four-track monophonic recorder, 120 minutes of recording time are available. A wide range of possible recording lengths is available. Common lengths are C-30, C-45, C-60, C-90, C-120 and C-180.

The *weather and age resistance* of a backing determines how long and how well a tape will stand up to time and to temperature and humidity changes. If the backing has poor weather and age resistance, the tape will not remain in good condition when temperatures and humidity are either at extremes or when they vary a great deal. On the other hand, good weather and age resistance means that the tape will not be easily damaged by these factors.

The tape backing must be *smooth* in order to take an even oxide coating essential to faithful reproduction. All backings have nearly equal smoothness characteristics.

The *flexibility* of the backing will also affect performance. The more supple the backing, the better its tape-to-head contact. This is critical for high frequencies and good volume in a recording. While tape backings differ in their flexibility, the thickness of the backing also plays its part. The thinner the backing, the better it will conform to the surface of the head.

The importance of the endurance factors may vary with the conditions of tape use. Neither good strength nor good weathering and aging characteristics may be needed for some circumstances. However, it would not be wise to compromise with the performance factors.

Using these criteria, we will evaluate the most popular tape backing materials used today: acetate, polyester, and PVC (polyvinyl chloride). The three base materials are used in open-reel tape, acetate being the most common. Among cassettes, polyester is nearly universal for reasons which will become apparent below. Because of this, cassette labels usually carry no description of the base material. The issue of which material a tape backing is made of becomes relevant and crucial only for open-reel tape.

How can you tell what backing material open-reel tape has?
For acetate, the label on the box may read either plastic, acetate, cellulose acetate, or triacetate. Polyester is usually
called simply polyester or Mylar, which is DuPont's name for the
polyester it makes and distributes to tape manufacturers. A PVC
backing may be identified by the name of polyvinyl chloride,
PVC, or Luvitherm (BASF's name).

If there is no label on the box, it is more difficult to tell
the various backings apart. Some differentiation can be made on
the basis of two simple tests which the tape detective should
keep in mind. The *light test* consists of holding a reel of tape
broadside to a light. If the tape is translucent, it is either
acetate or PVC; if it is opaque, the material is either polyester or PVC. By this test, acetate and polyester are separated
from each other, although neither is distinguished from PVC.
The *tear test* is performed by actually attempting to tear across
one layer of the tape. Acetate will snap apart with very little
stretching; polyester and PVC become deformed because they are
very resistant to tearing. This second test isolates acetate
from translucent PVC, but it does not distinguish PVC from polyester (Figure 10). Because polyester is so very common in the
United States, the probabilities are good that the opaque material is polyester. However, the lack of positive identifi-
cation is not so critical. Both PVC and polyester have nearly
identical characteristics.

LIGHT TEST

			Translucent	Opaque
T	T	Snaps	Acetate	
E	E			
A	S	Deforms	PVC	Polyester PVC
R	T			

Fig. 10. Two Tests to Determine Tape Backing Material

Acetate

Acetate is the most common and least expensive tape backing
for open reels of the three we are considering. Because it is
the weakest backing, it comes in 1 1/2-mil and 1-mil thicknesses
only. If the tape is bent or creased, the backing is weakened
at that point and will eventually break under nominal stress.
Whenever acetate breaks, however, the break is clean, with
little or no deformity by stretching. For this reason, some
tape users prefer to make their masters or original recordings

on acetate so that the pieces can be mended without loss of material when tape breakage occurs.

The really serious problems with acetate pertain to its aging and weathering characteristics. Acetate is made flexible by incorporating plasticizers into the base material. With time, however, the plasticizers dry out, and the tape becomes increasingly brittle. This loss of flexibility has several serious disadvantages. First, the tape will break even more easily than before. Second, the brittle tape will not conform well to the heads with a resultant loss of recording quality. Third, a dried out tape will often squeal as it passes across the heads of the recorder.

Weathering brings on even greater problems. Acetate has a tendency to expand with high temperatures and contract with low temperatures (called *creep*), so that the tape length will vary slightly from one time to the next. Humidity changes have even more serious effects. Low humidity will cause the tape to dry out faster than normal, while high humidity may cause it to deform. Absorbing the moisture in the humid air, acetate expands. The expanding layers press tighter and tighter against each other with the effect that the pressure forces the tape out of shape. Thus, the layers become thinner than 1 1/2 or 1 mil and wider than 1/4 inch. This deformity causes wow and flutter when the extra-wide tape binds on the tape guides of the recorder. Moisture absorption may continue even to the point of creating expansion pressure with such force that it will break the plastic reel hub on which the layers are wound. The longer dampness continues, the greater the chances that mildew will begin to grow on the tape.

Polyester

When compared with acetate, polyester is about ten times as strong. It has great advantages as open-reel and cassette tape. Its inherent strength has allowed the polyester backing to be reduced in thickness so that the available range of base thicknesses is from 1 1/2 mil to 1/4 mil and thinner.

Thinner tape brings with it the advantages that better tape-to-head contact is possible, and more tape can be wound on a tape reel for more recording time. The disadvantages of thin tape--stretching and print-through--are serious and should be considered.

First, rather than breaking cleanly, polyester will tend to stretch under stress. Not only does stretching deform the tape, but it also distorts the signal recorded on it. When the tape thickness is cut down, the propensity to stretch is even greater.

To combat this problem, some manufacturers prestretch their thin backing material. The *tensilized* polyester is consequently more resistant to stretching and provides a partial solution to this first disadvantage to thin tape.

> TIP: Before attempting to use open-reel tape of 1/2 mil thickness or C-120 or C-180 cassette tape, refer to Chapter 5 in the section on rough handling for pointers on how to manage ultrathin tape successfully. The problems which beset the thinnest cassette tape are especially serious.

The second disadvantage affects the tape's sound performance. As the backing is reduced in thickness, the phenomenon known as *print-through* increases. Print-through is the transfer of re- corded signals from one layer of tape to adjacent layers, cre- ating an echo effect. When recorded material is wound back onto the reel, the magnetized particles on a layer of tape begin to affect the sensitive oxide on adjacent tape layers, creating on that oxide small replicas of the signal. The signal has, in effect, printed through the backing to the oxide on the next layer above and below it. The thinner the backing, the more easily print-through occurs and the louder the effect. When the tape is played back, the signal will first be heard as an echo before the actual signal reaches the head. This is called the pre-echo. Then, after the signal passes the head, it appears again as a post-echo. Very strong signals have been known to create as many as ten audible echos by print-through. Further- more, each time the tape is played and rewound, new areas on adjacent layers are exposed to the recorded signals so that new print-through begins again. The result is an increasingly noisy tape.

Print-through has not been eliminated by any developments thus far in the recording industry. The control of print- through is achieved largely by the kind of oxide on the tape, the manner of recording, and certain storage precautions. These will be discussed under coating and recording tape care in Chapter 5.

As we have seen, the strength of polyester has its positive and negative features. Its age and weather resistance may be seen as a strictly positive feature. The polyester backing is very supple. Since it contains no plasticizers which eventually dry out, polyester keeps its flexibility indefinitely. Although this backing has been used for recording tape for a number of years, no one yet knows how long it will last. Besides showing no effects of age, polyester is also relatively impervious to humidity extremes and changes in temperature. These character- istics make it an ideal all-weather backing. It is particularly good for recordings that must be stored for long periods.

PVC

Polyvinyl chloride, the least common backing of the three under discussion, has many of the characteristics of polyester.
Its exceptional strength permits a wide range of backing thicknesses: 1 1/2, 1, and 1/2 mil. PVC is more flexible and somewhat more resistant to stretching than polyester. But like
polyester, *tensilizing* or prestretching is used by some companies to reduce the stretch problem.

PVC, too, is an all-weather backing unless exposed to temperatures of about 150° F or more, at which point it deteriorates.
By contrast, polyester will endure up to about 200° F. Few tape
users, however, will have reason to be concerned about such high
temperatures.

The distinct advantage PVC has over polyester for open-reel
tape is its price. It is less expensive than polyester with a
selling price closer to that of acetate.

Considering the characteristics of the three tape backings
discussed, we can offer the following recommendation.

TIP: Open-reel tape--For rough usage, long tape mileage per
reel, exposure to extreme climatic conditions, or long tape
storage, choose either a polyester or PVC backing. However,
proper caution should be exercised when using tape of 1/2-
mil thickness or thinner. For moderate use in a temperate
or controlled climate and for relative economy, acetate will
serve well for about five years.

Cassette tape--For a maximum of length with a minimum of
worry about reliability, we recommend C-90. C-120 and C-180
should be used only when there is no satisfactory alternative,
and when proper precautionary measures can be exercised.

Unlabeled or off-brand open-reel tape should be examined not
only for the type of base material used, but also for manufacturing flaws characteristic of poor quality tape. Tests for
flaws such as uneven slitting, irregular winding tension which
distorts the tape, and poor splices will be found in Appendix 3.
Unlabeled or off-brand cassette tapes are not recommended under
any circumstances, as discussed at the end of this chapter.

HOW WELL WILL TAPE COATINGS HOLD UP AND PERFORM?

The tape backing acts essentially as a carrier of the coating
that is spread on it. The coating is made up of millions of
microscopic needle-shaped iron particles, *oxide,* suspended in a
special glue called *binder*. The binder serves to separate each

needle from its neighbor and also to fasten the needles to the backing.

On open-reel tape, the coated side of the backing is found on the side closest to the reel hub. This is called an A-wind. B-wind is used on cassette tape, putting the oxide coating on the side opposite the reel hub. These differences reflect the location of the recording heads in the two types of machines.

The coating not only gives recording tape its physical color, but it also determines a tape's *acoustic color*--the quality of sound reproduction it is capable of. The physical color of the coating is the color of the oxide. This color is seen not only on the coated side of the tape (the dull side), but it is also visible on the opposite side (the shiny side) through the transparent backing. The acoustic color of the coating derives from the kind and amount of oxide that is mixed with the binder, how well it has been mixed, and how thickly and evenly the coating has been spread on the backing.

The *endurance* of a coating depends on (1) how well the coating adheres to the backing, and (2) how weather and age resistant the coating is. The *performance* of a coating is determined by (3) how smoothly the coating has been applied to the backing, and (4) what sound capabilities the oxide has. Each of these four characteristics will be considered in detail.

Coating-to-Base Adhesion

One of the most critical tasks in tape manufacturing is that of getting the oxide particles to stick on the very slick surface of the backing. If the coating is not fixed securely to the base material, it will flake off. Not only is recorded material lost and further recording impossible at that point, but the loose oxide, when it gets in the head gaps, will severely reduce record and playback quality.

In better quality tapes, manufacturers accomplish the costly task of good adhesion by putting a *primer* on the base material before applying the coating. The wearability, or resistance to deterioration through use, of a tape coating is greatly increased by the addition of a primer. It is relatively easy to determine whether or not a tape has been primed. If laid oxide-up on a smooth surface and scratched hard with the fingernail, the coating of a non-primed tape will come off, but a primed coating will stick firmly and resist removal. This test is not recommended for cassette tape.

Weather and Age Resistance

The binder is called on to do many jobs and do them well.
Individually, the jobs are not difficult, but when all of them
must be done at the same time and by the same substance, problems may arise. The binder must coat each oxide needle; it must
be thin enough to spread evenly; it must be super-strong to
stick to either the backing or primer; it must be dry yet remain
flexible; and it should be able to do these various jobs regardless of climate or age.

Inferior binders, however, will get gummy in high temperatures.
This will cause layers of tape to stick together. When the layers are unwound, the oxide may be pulled off the backing. Also,
the plasticizers and preservatives added to the binder may dry
out with changes in temperature. When this happens, the binder
becomes brittle and ill-suited to glide intimately across the
heads to receive or give back magnetic signals. As the additives begin to disappear, the binder will shrink. Cupping and
curling are likely to occur if the base material expands or
shrinks at a different rate from the coating.

Not all manufacturers have binders that will adequately do
all the jobs that binders must do under difficult circumstances.
Unless an unlabeled or off-brand tape is known to come from a
maker of name-brand tape, its binder may not be of the quality
needed to make the oxide coating sufficiently age and weather
resistant. For open-reel tapes, certain tests to determine
binder characteristics should be used. These tests will be
found in Appendix 3.

Smoothness

The difficulty involved in getting a smooth coating of oxide
on a tape backing has led to great differences in the quality of
the end product. We will look at what makes a tape smooth or
rough, how smoothness affects performance, and what extra efforts
some manufacturers make to insure smoothness.

A coating is smooth, first, by virtue of thorough mixing of
oxide and binder. If the mixing (milling) process is not long
enough, the magnetic needles will not be separated from each
other, but rather will clump together. When the coating is
applied to the backing, the clumps, called *agglomerates*, will
form bumps on the tape. Large agglomerates are visible to the
naked eye and are rough to the touch. The thoroughly milled
coating contains no agglomerates.

A coating is smooth, second, by virtue of uniform application
of coating to base or primer. A poor job of coating is easily

identified. A strip of tape held up to a strong light will reveal thin places, streaks in the coating, or even holes where no coating exists. Reputable tape manufacturers apply coating according to extremely exacting specifications. If a roll of tape is only minutely out of tolerance, it is not sold as top grade tape.

The oxide coating must be smooth for the sake of the recorder heads as well as for the sake of the quality of the recording. The tape acts as an abrasive as it moves across the recorder heads, wearing down the metal and destroying the critical dimensions of the head gaps. An open-reel tape recorder has to run only two and one-half hours at 7 1/2 ips for a mile-long piece of such sandpaper to rub across the heads. The rougher the oxide, the shorter the head life; the smoother the oxide, the longer the heads will wear. A badly worn head is incapable of delivering the frequency range of a comparable new head.

For best recording and playback performance, the tape must be in continuously intimate contact with the recorder heads. Imperfections in the tape, such as bumps, holes, or thin spots, modify the perfect contact and yield imperfect recording and playback results. An agglomerate lifts the tape away from the head so that both frequencies and volume are lost. A hole, of course, results in total loss of recording, while a thin spot will cause greater or smaller differences in volume. These effects, in which loss of one kind or another is sustained, are known as *dropout*. Dropout is especially noticeable on cassette tape where the 1 7/8 ips speed takes the hole, thin spot, or agglomerate past the head very slowly--four times more slowly than at 7 1/2 ips. Good quality recording tape is almost entirely free of dropout-causing defects.

Because of the degrading effects a rough tape surface can have on recording heads and recording quality, some tape makers take extra measures to insure smoothness. One method to do this is to *polish* the recording tape by brushing away loose oxide particles which might act as a bump on the tape, lodge in the gap of a recorder head, or etch the head as they are forced by.

Another process to control head wear is called *lubrication*. A dry lubricant such as silicone is incorporated into the tape binder before the coating is distributed over the backing material. Since a lubricant applied by this method lasts the life of the tape, it is a more effective anti-abrasive preparation than either polishing or external lubrication of tapes. Lubricants may also be incorporated into the backing material for flexibility, but these additives do not serve the cause of reducing head wear.

A third method to cut down abrasion is the application of an ultrathin layer of plastic over the oxide coating. Since the heads do not actually touch the coating, there is little head wear. There is, however, a slight loss in both high and low frequencies and volume.

A fourth measure is a carbon powder preparation incorporated into either the backing or the coating to prevent the buildup of static electricity which attracts dust and stray iron particles. Thus, a smooth, clean surface can remain that way.

These extra measures serve not only to protect the heads from rough oxide; they also protect the coating from deterioration through contact with tape guides, capstan, and heads, so that the coating itself lasts longer. Further protection of heads and coating may be gained by frequently cleaning the heads and tape guides.

TIP: For the sake of recorder heads, recording quality, and tape life, choose an anti-abrasion tape from a name-brand manufacturer. There is no bargain in poor quality coatings often found in *white-box* (unidentified) tape.

Sound Capabilities of Oxide

No other part of the recording tape, backing or coating, has been the locus for so many improvements as has the oxide. The advent of slower tape speeds, thinner tape backings, and narrower recording tracks brought problems which improved oxide coatings have been remarkably successful in solving. Researchers have been able to increase frequency response and volume output of a tape, as well as decrease background noise and the degree of print-through, all by means of manipulating the size and mag-netic characteristics of coating particles, altering the density of particles in the coating, and adjusting coating thickness on the backing.

The important thing to remember about selecting oxides is that the recorder and the tape must be compatible for the best recording results. Without some adjustments in the recorders, not all good tape will do equally well on all recorders. This situation derives essentially from the nature of tape recordings. Certain problems arise which are inherent in the job of putting recording signals on tape. The problems stem either from the *recording process* or from the *properties of recording tape.* Fortunately, ways have been discovered or devised to offset or make up for these problems electronically. One such compen-sation feature related to the recording process has been dis-cussed: equalization. A second compensation feature related more to the properties of the tape is called *bias*.[1]

Adjustments in equalization and bias are ordinarily preset in a recorder to deliver the best results for one kind of tape, usually a standard tape. When the characteristics of the tape are altered, for example, to yield lower noise or print-through, the tape recorder and tape are no longer compatible, unless the bias and/or equalization of the recorder are also altered to match the tape.

One writer has said that good recording performance is not so much a matter of picking the right tape as it is of making the right adjustment on the recorder to match the tape, whatever the tape may be.[2] This is certainly true for professional recordists who have machines that can be easily adjusted and who know how, and have professional reasons, to make the delicate adjustments needed. But for the nonprofessional recordist, good recording quality still depends largely on picking the right tape--a tape which will do the job at hand well and is also compatible with the existing adjustments of the recorder.

The bias and equalization settings of some recorders cannot be altered easily. But even where adjustments are provided for, only a professional tape recorder serviceman who has the appropriate instruments should make the adjustments. Not all recording tapes require special adjustment. Among the tapes discussed below, those that do require tape recorder adjustment will be mentioned.

In this section, we will look at oxides found in good quality tape. Since coatings on open-reel and cassette tape have different performance requirements, each of the two types of tape has its own set of oxides. Space is given to each set.

Open-Reel Tape Oxides. The oxides described here may be applied to any tape backing--acetate, polyester, or PVC. Special oxides, however, are used when the backing is ultrathin as in double- or triple-play tapes. Even though they are used in thinner coatings, these special oxides have characteristics which are similar to those of standard oxide. However, such coatings will generally deliver better high frequencies, lower print-through, but also lower output than standard oxide.

1. Standard Oxide. Nearly all major tape makers manufacture a tape with an oxide considered to have standard characteristics --a particular frequency response, output level, noise level, degree of print-through, and so forth. Most tape recorders are preset to function best with standard tape.[3] The assumption behind this setting is that standard tape is likely to be the kind most often used on the recorder. Certain facts support this choice. First, even though standard tapes are made by different companies, the properties of the various standards are very

similar. Second, the standard tape is often the most economical tape a company offers in its line of good-quality tapes. Third, the oxide yields very good results for general recording.

2. High-Output Oxide. When compared with standard oxide, the high-output coating offers improvements in a number of characteristics. First, stronger signals can be recorded without distortion; second, the oxide is more sensitive to weak signals; third, on playback, a stronger output is possible; fourth, the oxide has a better frequency response especially in high frequencies; fifth, the signal-to-noise ratio is greater; and sixth, the oxide has slightly better print-through characteristics. In short, high-output oxide does everything that standard oxide does, but in almost every case, the improved oxide does it better.

It has been estimated that eighty percent or more of all recording needs can be met satisfactorily with this tape oxide. It is especially good where demands are high, such as in slow-speed recording, narrow-track recording, and in recording very loud signals. The most important feature for the average tape user is that no recorder adjustments are normally necessary before using this oxide. It is compatible with settings for most standard tapes.

3. Low-Noise Oxide. Low-noise coatings were designed to attack the problem of bothersome hiss which comes from tape characteristics. This kind of noise is especially noticeable in tape duplicating and in slow-speed and narrow-track recording. Because low-noise oxide yields a better signal-to-noise ratio by several decibels than standard oxide, manufacturers recommend this coating for these special uses.

For best results, both bias and equalization should be readjusted. Some manufacturers, however, say that adjustments are not absolutely necessary for nonprofessional use. Without adjustments, low-noise oxide will reduce hiss by about three decibels and slightly extend the high-frequency range. With adjustments, improvement of five to six decibels is possible. An added benefit of this oxide is that it does not deteriorate, having greater wearability than standard oxides and does not wear the heads as greatly.

4. Low-Noise/High-Output Oxide. An oxide which combines the positive features of low hiss level and greater sensitivity and receptivity to higher record levels is one of the later additions to the set of open-reel tapes. It comes largely as a result of research done on oxides for cassette tape. The oxide is smaller and more consistent in shape than other oxides so that it can be dispersed more densely in the binder. As with low-noise oxides,

recorder adjustments are required in order to benefit from the features this tape offers.

5. Low-Print Oxide. Print-through is an effect that plagues all tape recordings. The longer a tape is allowed to remain wound on the reel without being played, the more pronounced print-through becomes. For this reason, it is especially noticeable in recordings which are intended for long storage such as in archival use. It is also a problem in tape masters which are used for duplicating purposes, because print-through effects are transferred to the copies in the duplicating process.

Since print-through results in part from the thickness of tape backings, sensitivity of magnetic oxide, and the strength of recorded signals, measures are taken by the manufacturer to minimize each contributing factor. The first step taken to reduce print-through is to spread the oxide on the thickest tape backing available, 1 1/2 mil. Besides using a different oxide composition, manufacturers also apply a thinner-than-ordinary coating of oxide to the base material. This means that the oxide is less sensitive over-all and is less receptive to strong signals. While these changes do not eliminate print-through, they substantially reduce its prominence.[4] In order to appreciate the value of low-print oxide, the recorder bias adjustment must be carefully tuned to the characteristics of this oxide.

TIP: Special tape recorder adjustment is not necessary in order to get superb tape recording results. We recommend standard oxide tape for good quality general recording. Tape with high-output oxide may be used for the highest quality in all kinds of recording jobs.

It should be noted that tapes from different name-brand tape makers will differ in their magnetic characteristics. For example, a high-output tape from one manufacturer may be noisier than the same tape type from another manufacturer. To assure yourself that you are choosing a tape which will function best on your recorder with the adjustments set as they are, there is a simple ear test that can be performed.

Splice together several 30-second-long sections of tape from different manufacturers, putting a leader between each section in order to identify each tape by brand and type. Then make two recordings. First, record with the record volume turned to zero. Second, flip the experimental tape over and record interstation noise from the FM band. To evaluate the tape sections, listen for the segment which gives you the *least* hiss from the first recording *and* which gives you the *clearest* and *loudest* reproduction of the noise from the second recording. This brand and type of tape will be best suited for your recorder set as it is.

Without special test equipment, it is difficult to know what kind of oxide an unlabeled tape has. Often the oxide will not fit any of the categories above. On the one hand, the tape may simply have such poor quality coating that it does not meet the minimum specifications of standard tape. On the other hand, the oxide may have been originally designed for different purposes, such as for computer or instrumentation tape. Oxide for these uses is well suited for high frequencies but has poor bass response. If you have performed the ear test suggested above and have isolated a good name-brand tape for your recorder, this tape can be compared in the same way with the unknown tape. While this will give you a clear indication of noise and output level, there is no assurance that the next box of the same off-brand tape will contain the same kind of tape. Not all oxide on off-brand or unlabeled tape is of poor quality; it is simply unpredictable.

Cassette Tape Oxides. The recognition by the recording industry that cassette recorders can potentially deliver high-fidelity sound has done more than anything else to stimulate research into oxides. Striking improvements have resulted, and most of them are found exclusively among cassette tapes. Since excellent results can be achieved on multi-speed, wide-track, open-reel recorders without these improvements, few of the new oxide compositions have appeared in the open-reel tape. The different needs of the two types of recorders have resulted in a different set of oxides for each type.

1. Standard Oxide. Each name-brand manufacturer has one tape which is taken as the reference point for evaluating the characteristics of its other oxides. Standard oxide coatings on cassette tapes in many cases have the magnetic characteristics we see in low-noise tapes for open-reel recorders. This is encouraging, since one of the key problems to be overcome by the cassette medium is noise. Many cassette recorders are preset for a standard oxide tape. If such care has been taken, the manufacturer will indicate which brand of tape has been used.

2. Low-Noise Oxide. Low-noise oxide for cassettes behaves much like low-noise/high-output tape for open-reel machines. The oxide particles are smaller than those used for standard oxide and this yields a lower amount of hiss than we see in standard oxide tape, registered as a greater signal-to-noise ratio. Since no recorder adjustments are necessary in order to use this coating composition effectively, low-noise oxide is a good choice for important recordings. It will even make a difference when used on old or inexpensive machines with low signal-to-noise ratios.

3. Low-Noise/High-Output Oxide. By using smaller oxide particles than found in standard oxide and by packing the particles

more densely into the coating, a number of major improvements in
performance have been achieved. A dramatic drop in the noise
level has come about with the smaller sized particles. Higher
recording levels can also be used without distortion which in
turn helps the noise problem. Since the input volume can be
greater, the playback volume can be lower. This decreases even
further the perception of noise. The more highly packed surface
of the coating allows the high frequencies to be preserved--one
answer to the chronic problem of self-erasure of highs which
comes with a slow recording speed. As is generally the case
with low-noise oxides, they are also less damaging to the recorder heads than standard oxides.

One of the meanings of high output is increased sensitivity.
A striking demonstration of sensitivity can be had when compar-
ing low-noise/high-output oxide with standard oxide. Record a
passage of music at the same input volume on a sample of each
tape type. Then play the two tapes at the same playback level.
The high-output oxide will sound noticeably louder.

The oxide discussed here can be used effectively on cassette
recorders with standard settings, although performance can usually be improved by having the settings optimized for a particular brand of tape.

Intensive research done with the basic gamma ferric oxide has
perfected its size and shape so that even greater particle density can be achieved than with low-noise/high-output tape. The
result is that this oxide surpasses all other gamma ferric oxides
in every category of performance and provides quality competitive
with chromium dioxide, discussed below. In order to maximize
the capabilities of this oxide for your recorder, adjustments
must be made, although improvement over standard oxide is noticeable even when no adjustments are made.

4. Chromium Dioxide (CrO_2). DuPont introduced a synthetic
compound into the recording tape industry which offers an extended high frequency response and a significantly lower noise
level than standard oxide tape. The new material is now available from every tape manufacturer at a cost of about double that
of standard tape.

To take advantage of the sound capabilities of this oxide,
the bias and equalization of the cassette recorder must be reset
since chromium dioxide is harder to magnetize and harder to erase
once magnetized than ferric oxide compositions. To accommodate
this tape and leave the recordist the option of using other
oxides, many cassette decks have two or three switches which adjust the electronics of the recorder to the demands of the tape
at hand.

Because adjustment switches are not found on many portable cassette machines, CrO_2 tape is off-limits for many language recordists. We should not be disappointed, however; equal or near-equal quality is available from some ferric oxides. Developments in ferric oxides have out-distanced improvements in CrO_2 and, thus, tape oxides, such as the improved low-noise/high-output oxide discussed above, can compete with the chromium dioxide tape without necessitating readjustments of equipment.

Nearly every manufacturer of tape offers the four types of oxide discussed above. The shopper should also be aware of other coating preparations available from some tape makers. They consist of ferric oxide modified by cobalt or magnetite. These impurities increase output and also appear to increase the signal-to-noise ratio over standard oxide. However, the oxide demands major recorder adjustments as does CrO_2 and will not be important for most language recordists for that reason. Ultimately, it offers little that cannot be attained through premium ferric oxides.

TIP: The problems inherent in slow-speed and narrow-track recording make recorder adjustments more important for cassette machines than for open-reel machines. However, optimizing adjustments is recommended only for those who must have the highest quality of reproduction, as for recordings which will undergo instrumental analysis. If this describes your needs, select a premium (low-noise/high-output) tape and have a competent serviceman adjust your recorder for it.

For most language recordists whose requirements are high but not those of the perfectionist, our recommendation is to use the type of tape recommended by the maker of your cassette machine (usually a standard or a low-noise oxide) for most purposes. For superior results, use a low-noise/high-output tape. Since your tape recorder will reproduce sound differently on name-brand tape of different manufacturers, it will pay to compare the quality available from several brands of low-noise tape or several brands of low-noise/high-output tape. Record a disc onto each of the several tapes you are testing. Then compare each tape with the original sound on playback, switching rapidly between tape and record. This can be done easily by operating the volume knob of each audio component. Listen in particular for hiss level, output level, clarity. If the differences are noticeable, choose the best tape. If the differences are imperceptible or very minimal, choose the least expensive tape.

NAME-BRAND AND OFF-BRAND TAPE

Throughout this chapter on recording tape selection, we have
drawn a distinction between superior and poor tape characteristics. The distinction has, in general, separated what we call
name-brand or house-brand tape from off-brand or *white-box* tape.
The boundary in quality between the two is not in fact so neatly
demarcated. But whether it is worthwhile to examine off-brand
tape to determine on which side of the quality boundary it falls
depends on whether it is open-reel or cassette.

The Case for Open-Reel Tape

The fact that some good quality recording tape is available
in unlabeled or relabeled boxes and the fact that open-reel recorders can tolerate greater variation in quality are the principal justifications for considering off-brand open-reel tape.
In dealing with such tape, it will pay to proceed cautiously.

Many of the anonymous characteristics of white-box tape can
be determined with some accuracy by using the various tests we
have suggested. But these simple tests cannot reveal everything. If you know the source of the white-box tape you are
considering, it is often possible to reject it immediately.
Guidance on this point may be found in Appendix 4. When
you feel you have found a real bargain--good quality tape at a
low price--buy a reel and put it through every test you know before investing in more reels.

Even when you find what appears to be good quality tape, remember that the chances are very good that it is defective in
some respect, however minor. It would not be wise to put your
best recordings on it. Use a name-brand tape for such recordings.[5] In this way, you have the assurance that your material
will not be affected by faults in the tape. Much of the extra
cost of name-brand tape is for the quality control exercised in
its production both in the choice and the assembling of materials.

Intermediate in savings between name-brand and off-brand tape
is house-brand tape marketed by major electronics distributing
companies under their own name. The advantage of house-brand
tape over off-brand tape is that it is reliable. Its characteristics are known and remain consistent from one box to the next.
In many cases, the tape is produced by a name-brand manufacturer.

The Case for Cassette Tape

Compared with open-reel machines, cassette recorders have
little tolerance for irregularities in tape. Compared with open-
reel tape, there are two major sources of irregularities among

cassettes, not one: the tape itself and the case. Off-brand tape compromises in both areas and is not recommended for the language recordist.

Cassette tape, as we have noted, must meet very exacting standards in order to yield good recording on narrow tracks and at a slow speed. Intolerable for good performance are the often-found rough-textured coatings and the coatings which shed their oxide. Both problems interfere with close tape-head contact and are causes of low volume, loss of high frequencies, and dropout. Within the cassette housing itself, debris can damage heads, collect on recorder parts and cause the tape to wind out of the cassette, wrap around capstan or roller and pack into the cassette machine. If the tape width is inconsistent, proper tracking cannot be maintained and the head will lay down tracks over those already present and play back tracks adjacent to the target track (crosstalk).

Cassette cases are a second source of problems because of their unreliability. They are often found to be poorly constructed, so that tape pulls away from the hubs, spindles are not free-turning and jam, guide posts promote wear, and pressure pads cause uneven wear on the heads. The two halves should fit precisely together. When they do not, the tape can slip out of the slit between the shell halves and snarl. Burrs and loose plastic particles inside the housing can jam tape movement and cause the tape to stretch or break.

In short, there is no bargain in *economy* cassette tape which bears an off-brand name or no name at all. A better way to economize is to use house-brand tape. House-brand tape is sold by large electronics distributing firms, such as Lafayette, Radio Shack, Team. Its characteristics are known and its price is moderate. If a quantity of tape is needed, as for use overseas where tape is very expensive or unavailable, even name-brand tape can be had at considerable savings if bought in large lots.[6]

5 Recording Tape Care

Recording tape and the signal on it are delicate. It takes very little to ruin either. Improper care or neglect can quickly lead to loss of backing, coating, or signal.

PROTECTING THE BACKING

The backing can be damaged by creasing, rough handling, and certain environmental factors. We will look at some safety precautions to take in order to protect the backing from such damage. Measures especially for open-reel or cassette tape will be indicated throughout the text.

Creasing

Creasing is not a problem for cassette tape housed in good quality cases. Since no loose ends of tape protrude from the case and no threading is required, the tape remains relatively damage free. For open-reel tape, however, the story is quite different. Acetate-backed tape in particular is susceptible to damage by creasing.

There are three common causes of creasing. First, the outside ends of the tape can be bent and crushed in the tape box when the end is left free. Second, when threading the tape or allowing it to flap when it has emptied the supply reel, the recordist will damage the ends. Third, if the tape is unevenly wound on the reel, the protruding edges of the tape may be creased longitudinally when the flanges are squeezed together. Care when handling the reels will solve this latter problem.

Tape Clip or Spongie. The solution to in-box creasing is the
tape clip or *spongie*. Usually made of plastic, the clip is
either attached to the tape and secured between the flanges of
the reel or else clipped to one side of the reel and pressed
against the tape windings. A second method of holding the tape
end close to the reel is the spongie, a one-half-inch cube of
sponge rubber or polyurethane foam. The spongie is pressed between the flanges of the reel against the tape. With a pair of
scissors, you can easily make your own spongies.

Leader Tape. Leader tape, a sturdy non-magnetic polyester
tape, prevents creasing of the recording tape during threading.
A piece of leader about eighteen inches long spliced onto each
end of a reel of tape can take repeated threading and a great
deal of flapping with no bad effects.

Leader tape has other valuable uses besides protection from
creasing. It is handy for labeling the contents of a reel. The
surface of the leader tape can ordinarily be labeled with a ballpoint pen or a permanent felt-tip marker. By splicing leader
segments within a reel of tape to mark sections, it may be used
as a cueing device for one-track recording. It is easy to identify tape sides or ends if a different color leader is attached
to each end. By this method, it is also easy to tell whether a
tape has been rewound onto the correct reel. When spliced onto
the end of the magnetic tape, the leader is sometimes called the
trailer.

Some leader tape is marked off in seven and one-half-inch or
three and three-quarter-inch sections. This is a handy aid for
timing pauses in editing. At 7 1/2 ips a seven and one-half-
inch length of leader represents one second. Provided only one
track of recording is used, very precise timing can be done with
such leader insertions. A simple scheme is given in Appendix 5
for determining how many inches of leader, marked or unmarked,
or recording tape must be cut out or added in order to shorten
or lengthen silent spaces.

When recording, it is possible to avoid initial clicks when
entering the record mode by using leader tape. If the recorder
is placed in record mode while the nonmagnetic leader is opposite the head, no click will be picked up. Furthermore, the
presence of a long leader going to the take-up reel permits the
recordist to begin recording very close to the beginning of the
magnetic tape. In this way there is little waste of tape time
at the beginning of a reel.

Warped Reels. Unfortunately, warped reels are more the rule
than the exception. Not only do they cause poor tape feeding
and winding, but they also take their toll from the recording

tape itself. If the tape touches the reel flanges while in
motion, the edges of the tape will be frayed and oxide loosened.
Layers of frayed tape cannot track evenly, giving uneven pressure
on the tape. The remedy: Replace warped reels so that they become the exception rather than the rule in your recording library.

TIP: Insist on reels that are true, always use some device
to secure the outside end of open-reel tape while not in use,
and always use leader on both ends of every reel of tape.

Rough Handling

Tape can be broken, stretched, or deformed through rough
treatment by the recorder, both open-reel and cassette. Thin
tape--1/2 mil or thinner--cannot be used successfully on all
machines. Transport systems differ in how kindly they treat
tape.

In open-reel tape, caution must be exercised when using 1/2-
mil tape, especially nontensilized polyester. Starting and
stopping the tape recorder can stretch the tape if the machine
is poorly adjusted. Single AC-motor machines are particularly
prone to have this problem; multiple-motor and DC-motor recorders tend to be kinder to thin tape. See Chapter 1, page 47 for
a test to see whether this kind of tape can be used safely on
your machine.

If the recorder does not maintain proper tension on the tape
during all operations, the tape may get out of place and may
break, stretch, or crease if it is wound between the reel and
the turntable or between the reel flange and tape windings. The
remedy is to adjust the tension on the recorder so that it functions properly.

Some recorders tend to wind the tape too tightly onto the
reel. This causes such a buildup of pressure on inside windings
that the layers are pressed out of shape. This difficulty is
especially serious when running the tape in fast forward or reverse. Fast speeds use more tension in tape winding than is
used in playback or record speeds. A tape should not be stored
after fast winding, but should be allowed to wind loosely onto
the original reel before storage. If both sides of a tape are
played, proper winding will take place naturally. But if only
one side of a tape is used, or if a second side is not completed,
rewinding should be done at the fastest ips speed, not fast forward or reverse. Such rewinding not only results in proper tape
tension on the reel, but it also insures more even winding with
each layer exactly over the last one. Before rewinding, a thin
plastic shim can be slipped between the head and tape to prevent
unnecessary head wear.

TIP: In summary, determine whether or not your recorder can
use thin open-reel tape. Check or adjust the recorder for
proper tension so the tape does not spill off the reels.
Finally, avoid storing tape after fast winding.

Ultrathin cassette tape presents problems the user should be
aware of. Problems arise especially with C-120 and C-180 cassettes. The backing of these tapes is 1/4 mil or thinner and is
subject to many more ailments than the thicker tape.

Before using ultrathin tape for serious purposes, assure yourself that your machine can handle it by running the test referred
to above on your tape. If no problems arise, then you will want
to make the wisest and safest use of thin tape when you have it
on your machine. Certain facts and precautions can help. Recordings on ultrathin tape have noticeably more wow and flutter
than recordings made on thicker backings. While there is nothing
that can eliminate this problem, it can be minimized and your
tape protected by taking the following measures. Be sure that
the tape is wound tightly between the reels before using it.
Tightening the tape can be done manually by rotating the hub of
one reel until tension is restored. Loosely wound tape can
quickly wrap around the capstan, break or pack into your machine.
Any bit of gum or dampness on the rubber roller can catch the
thin tape and snarl it around the roller in short order. So
keep the roller clean as suggested in Chapter 2. Since even a
fingerprint on the oxide can cause significant dropout (loss of
signal quality and strength), avoid handling the tape itself.
To guard against stretching, fast forward and reverse speeds
should be used only with great care, and switching rapidly from
one to the other should never be done. Finally, keep an eye on
the recorder when in operation.

Environmental Factors

We have mentioned earlier that humidity and temperature extremes can be especially damaging to acetate base material and
inferior binder composition. Ideal conditions would require all
tape to be used and stored at 70° F and 50 percent relative humidity the year round. Such conditions are obviously impractical
for the majority of tape users. Rather, the precaution to take
is to avoid extreme temperatures--hot or cold. The glove com-
partment or trunk of a car, for instance, is no place for recording tape. In very humid areas, as in the tropics, keep
tape in a dehumidifying container with the recorder. As we have
suggested, only polyester or PVC should be used in areas where
adverse climatic conditions are prevalent. If, by chance, an
acetate tape is exposed to extreme humidity, it should be
allowed to remain in average humidity for at least twelve hours
before use.

PROTECTING THE COATING

Like the backing, the oxide coating which bears the signal
should be protected from harm. The aim of coating care is to
insure that the coating will not be separated from the backing.
The measures suggested here apply equally to open-reel and
cassette tape.

Aside from poor coating-base adhesion, there are several ways
to lose the coating. It can be damaged by many of the same factors which damage the tape backing. By repeatedly passing over
recorder parts, the coating may be scratched off slowly. It may
chip or flake off when unwinding layers which are stuck together.

Some simple precautions can forestall these kinds of damage.
Recorder parts which are in contact with the head do not have to
be rough to wear away the oxide coating. In general, the life
of the tape is prolonged if the recorder parts--heads, guides,
lifters--are cleaned frequently with the special solvent compound mentioned in Chapter 2 in the section on head maintenance.
This will facilitate the tape in gliding easily over these metal
surfaces. Of course, if there is a true rough place on one of
these parts, the tape coating will bear telltale evidence of it.
Running parallel with the path of the tape, striations or scratch
marks will be noticeable on the coating. By holding the tape to
a light, severe scratching will show up as thin places or streaks.
If you suspect such damage to your cassette tape, be very cau-
tious when checking it. A toothpick can be used to pull the
tape from the case. Then be careful not to touch the oxide with
bare fingers. Whatever recorder part is causing the scratching
should be cleaned or replaced immediately.

The use of a bulk eraser for erasing whole reels or cassettes
will cut down substantially on unnecessary contact of the tape
coating with recorder parts. The operation of the bulk eraser
is described in Chapter 2.

Two precautions against creasing have been mentioned for open-
reel tape: use tape clips and leader tape. Since stretching
will also cause the oxide to loosen, follow the suggestions given
earlier for preventing stretching which results from using ultrathin tape on a transport system which cannot handle it: Adjust
the recorder or stop using thin tape.

Excessive heat and humidity have an ill effect on coatings.
Hot temperatures (above 100° F) tend to make the coating binder
tacky. As the layers of tape press against neighboring layers,
the coating may stick as tightly to the adjacent backing as it
does to its own backing. Excessive humidity may create similar

effects. Humidity deposits moisture between tape layers and causes the layers themselves to expand. With expansion, the damp layers, in effect, are cemented together. When the reel of tape is later used, the windings that are bonded together tear apart and take with them bits of coating from other layers. To avoid such ill effects, follow the guidelines that have been suggested above for protecting the backing.

PROTECTING THE SIGNAL

The purpose of protecting the backing and the coating is ultimately to protect the signal on it. If the backing deteriorates, the coating and signal will also be lost. When the backing and coating remain intact, the signal will last indefinitely long provided it is not damaged by external and internal magnetic fields. External magnetic fields created by electric motors, televisions, air conditioners, bulk erasers, head demagnetizers, florescent light, and even nondemagnetized heads, can effectively erase a signal, reduce its strength, or add static to the tape. Internal magnetic fields refer to the effect of strong magnets on the tape--the signals themselves-- which print through the backing material and degrade the signal with echo and noise. In order to protect the signal on open- reel and cassette tape, both of these menaces must be controlled to a large extent.

External Magnetic Fields

The only real protection from external magnetic fields is to keep adequate distance between the tape and external magnetism. As mentioned above, this means careful use of both the head de- magnetizer and the bulk eraser. Further precaution should be exercised when storing tape to be certain the location is not adjacent to any electrical field source.

Internal Magnetic Fields

In the previous chapter it was pointed out that if thick base material, thin oxide coating, and low record level are used, some of the factors contributing to print-through can be partially offset. The study of print-through has revealed that there are still other factors that play a part in printing. Print-through increases when tape is (1) tightly wound, (2) exposed to high temperatures, (3) exposed to external AC fields, and (4) left wound without playing for long periods of time. Many of these factors can be controlled by proper storage practices.

Preventative measures have been discussed which apply equally well to the first three factors. Besides preventing distortion,

loose tape winding decreases print-through. By avoiding high
temperatures, the drying out of tape lubricants and the tacki-
ness of binder are reduced, and so is print-through. By maintaining proper distance between tape and AC fields, not only is
the recorded signal protected from erasure and static, but
print-through can also be held to a minimum. Thus, certain precautions serve a number of protective functions.

Another cause of increased print-through is factor four: the
length of static contact of *master* and *slave* particles. One
measure which serves to break the static contact is to use the
tape frequently. A number of professional recordists practice
another preventative measure for their open-reel and cassette
tapes which are recorded on only one track. They store them
tails out. That is, the recordings are put away after playing
without rewinding to the beginning. Before playing the tapes
again, they must be rewound--an action which will noticeably reduce print-through effects. If tapes have been stored for six
months or more, they should be rewound before use.

Even if low-print oxide tape is not used, these precautions,
together with lower record level setting and avoidance of ultrathin tape, will improve the print-through resistance of your
recordings.

OTHER PROTECTIVE MEASURES

Three other good storage practices should be used. First,
reels of tape and cassettes should be stored in boxes. The box
itself will act as a buffer against temperature and humidity
changes. It will also protect the tape from dust which is an
abrasive not only to the recorder heads but to the tape coating
as well.

Second, boxes of tape should never be stacked one on top of
the other. Rather, it is a better practice to stand the boxes
on edge like library books. Stacking puts weight on the cassette
case or the reel flanges and causes the tape to feed poorly.

Finally, if you have master recordings from which you make
copies periodically, it is a good idea to keep masters out of
circulation. Constant use increases the risk of damaging the
backing, coating, or signal of the masters. The masters may
also pick up hiss and lose their high frequencies when played on
recorders with nondemagnetized heads. This noise, as we have
mentioned, will be compounded in the duplicating process.

Part Two

Operation of Recording Equipment

Introduction to Part Two

In Part One, we advocated that you choose your recording equipment on the basis of the recording quality you need. If you use this criterion, we may assume that you are also interested in making recordings equal in quality to the quality of your equipment.

To exploit the recording capabilities of your tools to the fullest involves becoming proficient in the art of operating recording equipment. Without a certain amount of expertise, tapes from the most judiciously selected and meticulously cared for equipment will sound only a little better than recordings from a dimestore special.

As with most skills, handling recording equipment can be learned with patience, practice, and a little know-how. In this part of *Tips on Taping*, we are concerned with the know-how involved in making the best use of our instruments and supplies. This concern leads us to consider two essential phases in the creation of any finished taped product: recording and editing.

Recording is the job of getting the original material on tape. This is the product *in the rough*. Editing is the job of refining the original to create a finished product. The two phases are complementary. The TIPS we provide throughout the following chapters should prove helpful to you in developing both of these essential skills.

6 General Recording Techniques

Some recording techniques apply to nearly all kinds of recording
situations; other techniques are somewhat more specialized.
Since the general techniques are basic to the successful recording of language materials, we will begin here. In anticipation
of the following chapter on language recording techniques, we
center our attention in this chapter largely on microphone recording. However, by copying sound directly from another instrument (such as a phonograph, radio, television, or another
tape recorder) using a connecting cable, recordings can be created without microphones. We will discuss mikeless recording
briefly at the end of this chapter.

   Whether you are using an open-reel or cassette recorder, the
production of an original recording with or without a microphone
demands two types of control from the operator: control over
unwanted sound--noise--and control over wanted sound--signal.

THE OTHERWISE PERFECT RECORDING

   In our simplified sketch of the recording process, we said
that sound consists of vibrating air waves that are translated
into equivalent electrical vibrations by the microphone. The
original sound, however, can be of two sorts: desirable and undesirable. Unfortunately, the mike does not know the difference
and performs its translation process indiscriminately upon all
incoming vibrations. Ultimately, these vibrations are printed
on the recording tape, and what would have been an otherwise
perfect recording ends up filled with noise.

Noise, defined as any unwanted sound, is the primary enemy of
tape recording. Not only does its presence label the recording
as amateurish, but noise also serves as an unusually irritating
distraction. A phenomenon known as *listener fatigue* is created
when the listener must pay attention to content (signal) gener-
ously interspersed with noise. When the listener's attention
must be constantly focused on the taped material, as when using
language drills or taking phonetic transcription, noise brings
on fatigue very quickly.

The control of noise requires much energy and care. The approach used for its control is to determine the noise sources,
then try to eliminate or neutralize them. Categorized broadly,
noise emanates from two basic sources. Each is discussed below.

Source One: External Noise Entering the Microphone

Examples of external noise are legion. For our purposes,
however, we will group them into four types: (1) noise from the
larger environment such as other voices, dogs barking, cars moving, chairs scraping, paper rustling, wind blowing; (2) noise in
the form of echos produced as a side effect of wanted sound;
(3) noise resulting from contact with the microphone; and
(4) noise from recorder operations, such as motor whirr, tape
squeals, scraping of reels in open-reel models, snaps of recorder
controls. In order to get on the tape, these four types of audible noise must enter the microphone.[1]

Source Two: Noise from Internal Functioning of the Recorder

Noise which is inaudible when it is produced can get on the
tape directly from the machine. We become aware of it only when
playing back a section of recording. Although a number of examples of this type of noise have been considered earlier, they
will be listed along with others: (1) noise created by the electrical functioning of the recorder measured as the ratio of
signal to noise; (2) noise, usually a click, produced when using
an electrical pause control during recording; (3) noise similar
to (2) above resulting from entering or leaving the record mode.

Having identified the principal sources of noise, we are
faced with the question of how to eliminate or neutralize these
sources.

CONTROLLING NOISE SOURCES

The use of a professional recording studio is the best solution for many of the external disturbances listed above. The
use of professional equipment would also eliminate many of the
internal noises. In the absence of such ideal conditions, the

job at hand is to replicate for your own situation as many characteristics of the ideal setting as possible. We set about,
then, to consider how to gain the greatest degree of control
over the noise sources we have described.

Source One: External Noise

Noise from the Larger Environment. Noise control is more
difficult for outdoor than for indoor recordings. We have suggested the use of a uni- or hyperdirectional microphone to narrow
the receiving area as much as possible in order to include only
the subject being recorded. By positioning the mike close (a
few inches) to the subject, a greater amount of wanted sound
volume will be present per volume of unwanted sound. Close mike-
mouth distance can be maintained best by attaching the mike to
a lavalier around the speaker's neck. Some microphones are
small enough to be pinned to the shirt or blouse, or to a lapel
or pocket for the same effect. In addition, a windscreen can be
purchased or constructed to fit around the microphone to avoid
the rushing sound made by the almost imperceptible movement of
wind currents across the face of the mike.[2]

For indoor recording, the secret to quiet surroundings may
often be as much a matter of timing as of selecting the right
place. If recording is to be done in a home setting, where
people are present, it may be helpful to alert them to what is
taking place. A note on the door may help prevent untimely and
distracting entries.

When the recordist is using a script, a major offender in the
effort to squelch noise is the crackle of paper. Certain measures can be used to avoid this disturbance. Program text should
be typed on only one side of each sheet so that it is not necessary to turn papers. Stiff paper--twenty-pound stock or greater
--is preferred so that it will not crackle when moved. Paper
can be inserted in clear plastic folders for the same effect.
When moving papers, they should be lifted to the side, not slid.
By turning up one or more corners of each sheet, the recordist
can easily get a grip on the page he wants and can avoid the
noise of trying to lift only one recalcitrant sheet.

If some advance preparations are made, noise is less likely
to come from those involved with the recording. First, it is
wise to have the recording strategy well mapped out ahead of
time so that all instructions given to the participants can be
explicit. A nonrecorded trial run should be made to see that
everyone involved understands his responsibility. Second, the
recordist and his subjects should agree on a simple system of
silent signals to use during the recording process. Hand signs
will often be needed to say such things as: Begin or stop

recording; Speak louder or more softly; Speed up or slow down
the tempo; It is your turn; and so forth. In these ways, need--
less, and often noisy, interruptions can be eliminated.

TIP: Even when the precautions suggested above have been
observed, our environment is still rarely absolutely quiet.
We will still be unable to escape the low rush of air in
cooling or heating sytems, or the buzz of florescent lights,
or the whirr of refrigerator or electric typewriter motors,
or the gurgle of water in pipes, or the distant noise of
activity, the low roar of traffic, the sounds of birds, or
the periodic cracks and pops of expanding and contracting
building materials. Nevertheless, if the noise is very
quiet, a high record level and a loud sound source can put
the noise far enough into the background to mask it effectively by contrast.

Echos. Even in the quietest indoor setting, the sounds
wanted for recording can be the very source of unwanted sounds
in the form of echos. In the presence of hard surfaces and bare
walls, sound vibrations will bounce here and there to re-enter
the microphone. To reduce echos, it is extremely important to
do your recording where there is some acoustical buffering surrounding the recording scene. A *live* room, alive with echos,
can be converted into a relatively *dead* room by using a rug or
carpet on the floor, drapes covering the windows, and upholstered
furniture. These soft surfaces will tend to absorb the echos.
If there are bare walls and no floor covering, it is advisable
to drape some sheets or blankets on chairs around the immediate
recording area to deaden some of the bouncing sound.

TIP: To determine whether a room is live, clap your hands
or emit a fast, short whistle. If you hear a crack from your
hands or an echo from your whistle just as you finish, you
have a live room. A little experimenting in different rooms
will sensitize you to room characteristics. If you are unable to dampen the echo sufficiently, record with the mike
very close to the sound source.

In any room, it is often helpful to make a short sample recording in various locations before starting to record. You
will usually find one spot which is more free from echos than
any other place in the room. A good rule to follow is to stay
at least four feet from any unbuffered wall when recording.

Contact with the Microphone. The first guide in handling the
microphone is DON'T--don't handle the mike. Unless it is specially protected, even the slightest touch to the microphone
housing will register with the pickup element and be transferred
to the tape as static or pops. Movement of the microphone from

speaker to speaker when recording will almost inevitably be picked up by the mike. If on-the-spot interviewing requires a hand-held mike, the handle should be padded and a windscreen attached.

Whenever possible, the microphone should be set in place and not touched. If the mike is on a table, it is best to put a cushion or towel under the mike to cut vibrations from the surface. A mike stand carved out of a sponge or foam rubber block can serve as a stand as well as a vibration buffer.[3] If the mike is on a lavalier, be sure that it will not come in contact with buttons, metal pins, or jewelry.

Recorder Noise. There are several kinds of recorder noise which must be controlled. Motor noise and extraneous metallic vibrations can be dampened (1) by not putting both recorder and microphone on the same hard surface, (2) by placing the recorder at a distance from the microphone, (3) by directing the microphone face away from the recorder, and (4) by covering the machine if the cover will not interfere with the operation or ventilation of the machine. Combinations of these methods should serve to muffle noises adequately.

Remedies should be sought for squeaking tape. On open-reel recorders a thorough cleaning or replacement of pressure pads, a cleaning of the heads, capstan, and tape guides, and a check for warped reels will probably relieve the problem of squeaking tape. If not, the trouble may be dried out tape. If a reel is scraping, check for a warped reel, a bent spindle, or uneven turntable.

On cassette machines, squeaking or squealing tape may be caused by dirty heads or capstan. The more likely source of the problem is in the cassette case where guides and pads may be dirty or the reel hubs are binding. Difficulties such as these are characteristic of off-brand cassettes which not only contain inferior tape but also use structurally and mechanically poor cases.

Proper management of the recorder controls can sometimes minimize the chances of loud, sharp, mechanical snaps appearing on the recording. When entering or leaving the record mode, the controls will make noise. If a manual volume control is being used, volume can be turned to zero when operating the buttons or levers so that the microphone will be deaf to noises of this sort. This measure is not available when using automatic volume control.

Source Two: Internal Noise

Electrical Functioning of Recorder. Recorder noise is
inherent in the particular machine used. Although nothing can
be done to eliminate it, it can be reduced by recording at a
faster speed. It can be covered up by using the proper recording volume. It can be kept from increasing measurably through
care of the machine.

Electrical Pause Control Clicks. There is little that can be
done to modify the effect of the electrical pause. If the pause
will be used in recording, it is a definite help to allow a
space before and after a click. In this way, editing out the
click will be made easier, and the possibility of removing good
material will be lessened.

Entering and Leaving Record Mode. A click-producing capability is nearly always present when changing to and from the
record function. To avoid the click at the beginning of a reel
of tape or a cassette, put the machine in record mode while the
leader tape is opposite the record head.

Some open-reel machines release the tape from its tight position against the heads and between the capstan and roller when
the mechanical pause is applied. If your machine is of this
type, another method to eliminate initial record-mode clicks is
available. Apply the pause before putting the recorder in record mode. Once in record mode, turn the tape back manually
several inches until the newly-created click is on the feed-reel
side of the erase head. In this way, when the pause is released,
the erase head will remove the click as the tape passes by.

One way to avoid all mode change clicks on open-reel tape is
to insert a small flat piece of plastic--like the pocket clip of
a ballpoint pen top--between the record head gap and the tape
when entering or leaving record mode.

If none of these procedures is possible, then allow three or
four seconds of blank tape to ride by after entering or before
leaving record mode. The click will be far enough away from the
recorded material that it can be removed easily.

The control of noise, which has been the focus of the above
discussion, applies during the recording process. While the
measures and suggestions offered here attack noise at its
sources, some noise still remains. The job of eliminating the
last traces of removable noise comes after recording is finished.
Postrecording control of noise is one aspect of editing, an important topic to be dealt with at length in Chapter 8. It should
be said here, however, that the greater the control of noise at
the time of recording, the easier the job of editing will be.

CONTROLLING SIGNAL INPUT

In a nonprofessional setting, the control of unwanted sound is decidedly more difficult than the control of wanted sound. Our efforts to control noise are hampered by the nature of noise itself--voluminous and unpredictable--and by our limited juris-diction over noise sources. By contrast, control of signal is largely in the hands of the operator. Signal is limited in quantity, predictable, and therefore, manageable. Its control consists basically of governing the amount of signal delivered to the tape.

In a simple recording operation, there are three points where the amount of signal to reach the tape may be affected: at the source, at the microphone, and at the recorder. At the source, we are concerned with loudness and clarity. At the microphone, we pay attention to distance and position relative to the source. At the recorder, we are interested in the input volume control. While other intermediate points can be introduced to affect the signal, we will focus on the problem of co-ordinating the three central variables.

In the chapter on microphones, Chapter 3, these same variables were discussed. There, microphone directionality was at issue. The choice of directionality was seen as dependent on the inter-relationship of the characteristics of the sound source and mic-rophone position and distance. Here, microphone directionality and the sound source are considered as the main factors affect-ing microphone placement. Since the same variables are involved, we refer the reader to the earlier discussion of direction of pickup for supplementary information.

Source Loudness and Clarity

In some situations the recorder operator is in a position to modify the performance of the subjects being recorded. In other situations, he is helpless to do so, but can often achieve the desired effect through mike placement and record level adjust-ments. In this section, we are concerned with the kinds of control that can be exercised over the source.

When there is only *one sound source*, the sound should repre-sent at least the normal expected loudness for that particular source. The human voice has a natural range of voice loudness. Soft-spoken persons in particular should be urged to use the upper portion of that range without straining their voices. A strained voice can be easily detected on a recording, and, be-cause it is tiring, it is difficult to maintain.

If there are *several sound sources*, for example, when various persons are talking or singing, there are two considerations to

bear in mind. Relevant to singing, one consideration is that
the clearest voice should be closest to the microphone so that
the words can be more easily recognized. Secondly, if there are
widely differing natural voice volumes in the group, participants should be alerted to bring their volumes closer together,
if possible. When such efforts fail to bring results, other
ways may be used to equalize the output differences. These
methods are discussed below.

Microphone Distance and Position

Any discussion of microphone placement should be tempered by
the reminder that microphone placement is more of an art than a
science. Any amateur recordist who has had some feeling of uncertainty about where to put his microphones should take heart
in the fact that professional recordists typically spend more
time setting up their equipment than they do actually recording.
This is not to say that microphone placement is all trial and
error. It is not. With a knowledge of certain fundamentals
about the interaction of microphone directionality and characteristics of the sound source, the recordist can remove most of
the error at the beginning. In fact, trial or experimentation
may not be necessary at all except for making some very fine
adjustments in microphone position.

Microphone placement for recording live music from either
single or multiple instruments requires an understanding of the
acoustic characteristics of the sound delivered by different
instruments. When voice is combined with musical accompaniment,
recording becomes more involved. Guidance in these matters is
not our central concern here, but it is not hard to find.[4] For
speech recording, however, we can present some general guidelines and TIPS for the control of this variable. In our discussion, we center on speech situations which are being recorded
with one or more unidirectional microphones.

For ordinary *single source* voice recordings, one microphone
is sufficient. It should be kept at a distance of about six
inches for a soft voice or about ten inches for normal or full
voice loudness. If the room in which recording takes place is
moderately *dead*, the distance between mike and subject might be
increased somewhat. The best way to establish the mike-mouth
distance is to suspend the mike on a lavalier about the speaker's
neck. Nothing more is needed than a cord of some kind attached
to the microphone with a rubber band.

When recording at close proximity to the speaker, a mike on a
table stand has a tendency to pick up and exaggerate certain
sounds such as aspiration, breathing, and the hiss of some consonants. To reduce this effect, put a windscreen over the mike

face. If the problem is not eliminated, turn the face of the
mike slightly to the side so that the speaker is not talking
directly into it. To use this effect to advantage—for example,
to distinguish fine phonetic features—do just the opposite.
Remove the windscreen and position the mike exactly in front of
the speaker's mouth.

If there are *different sources* being recorded at the same
time, several possibilities are open for the number and placement of microphones. When a large group is taped, two or more
microphones can serve to capture a representative selection of
sound. One effective way of arranging two mikes on a stand or
table is to locate the pickup ends seven to eight inches apart
and pull the base of the mikes together so that they form an
angle of about 110 degrees. Another arrangement is to place the
mikes at separate points on the floor, pickup ends directed
toward the sound source.

TIP: In cases where considerable microphone cable will be
used, be sure to tape the cable to the floor with masking
tape so that it will not be tripped over.

When two persons are involved as sound sources, two mikes,
especially if lavaliers, can serve to balance their volumes and
will deliver far better results than a one-mike arrangement.

When multiple microphones are used, as in the situations just
discussed, there are several ways the sound may reach the recorder. The lines can run to a mixer, a central connection box
with an individual volume control for each input line and an
output line (or two) leading to the recorder. Or, if a four-
track stereo (or mono/stereo) recorder is being used with only
two microphones, each line can go to its own channel in the recorder. Because of problems with impedance, it is not possible
simply to merge mike lines together at a Y-connector and go from
there to the recorder without degrading the recording quality.

A second possibility for recording different sources is to
use only one mike. While one mike is not ideal, it is often all
the recordist has on hand. By positioning the mike on a boom
above and to the front of a group, an effective representation
of sound is possible. For monophonic recording of a group, some
recording authorities prefer one mike instead of two. Since
there is no depth in monophonic recording, the one mike will reproduce sounds more like they would be heard by one's own ears,
with a natural balance of parts. For using one mike with only
two persons, the participants should be seated close together so
that the pickup pattern of the mike can intercept both voices.
If one voice is stronger than the other, the mike should be
moved in the direction of the weaker voice.

Volume Control

Volume control, the third variable, is intentionally placed
last. It is easy to think that volume control is at the heart
of good recording. The fact is, however, that volume control
only complements the first two variables--source loudness and
mike distance and position. If these have been properly managed,
the volume adjustment will ordinarily be easy to make. If these
have not been properly managed, the volume control will not always be able to compensate for poor handling of the other
factors.

If automatic volume control (AVC) is being used, a flick of
the automatic control switch is not the way to recording success.
The term *automatic* should not be deceiving. This control takes
care of volume only after it has entered the machine. It does
not automatically assure a perfect recording when the source is
not sufficiently loud or when the microphone is not near enough
to the source. The effectiveness of this control depends ultimately on the first two variables. If manual control is being
used, the operator must remember that this control, too, must
work co-operatively with the other two variables.

What is the ideal record level setting? Tape recorder manuals
are notoriously vague about this matter. The advice most often
heard from recorder manufacturers is to experiment. This is
good advice, however, only (1) if the recordist knows exactly
what kind of results he wants from his experiment, and (2) if he
knows *how to experiment* to get the results he wants. Without
these two basic bits of knowledge, the recommendation to experiment leaves the recordist little better off than he was before
such advice. There is no need to be so vague in the matter of
finding the proper record level. What is required is that the
two questions above be answered clearly.

First, what kind of results does the recordist look for?
What is the goal of his experimenting with record volume? Essentially, he is looking for a setting between two extremes. He
would like to avoid putting too much volume on the tape because
too much volume causes the sound to be distorted and to be partially or totally unintelligible. He would also like to avoid
recording too little volume on the tape. Too little volume will
not cover up the recorder hiss that gets on the tape as an inevitable part of recording.

The reason is obvious for avoiding volume which is too strong.
But the reason weak volume is undesirable may not be so clear.
Besides being objectionable in itself, hiss can obscure phonetic

details in language material. This can be especially damaging
for pronunciation drill material used in language learning and
for field data which must be transcribed or subjected to instrumental analysis. Hiss is also damaging for master recordings
which will be copied onto other tapes (using two tape recorders).
Audible hiss will be greatly magnified in the copies. In order
to make a good copy, the volume of the master machine must be
turned up so that the signal will be loud enough. When this is
done, the hiss also becomes louder. To this hiss is added the
hiss of the slave machine as it records the tape. The resulting
copy is therefore much noisier than the original recording.

The ideal record level setting--and the goal of experimenting
--is a setting which permits volume which is low enough to avoid
distortion but high enough to mask recorder hiss. This rule applies for automatic volume control as well as for manual record
control.

Automatic volume control is designed to restrict volume to
this safe zone between the extremes. Excessive incoming volume
is moderated, while weak volume is somewhat boosted. If source
loudness and mike distance and position are correct, AVC will
perform in the desired fashion. The only way to know whether it
is possible to get a good recording with AVC is to make a trial-
run recording. A trial run consists of recording a few minutes
of material, and then listening to it at one-third to one-half
full playback volume to see if the results are satisfactory. If
by chance the recording is not loud enough, the problem rests
with the source and/or the mike distance. The solution is either
to (1) increase the source loudness; (2) move the mike closer to
the source; or (3) if neither of the above suggestions is possible, or if neither yields good results, then the recording should be tried using manual control if available.

The second question about experimenting is this: How does
the recordist go about finding the safe-zone setting manually?
The trial-run procedure given below will work for *any* recorder
in which the record level can be controlled manually. The procedure is given in detail and in step-by-step form because getting the correct record volume is of such crucial importance.

The aim of the trial-run procedure is the following: *To record language and speech material (spoken at normal conversa-
tional loudness) so that, when you play it back at one-third
playback volume, the recorded voice will sound as loud as the
voice was when recording.*

1. Set the record level at one-half full volume.

2. Position the mike about eight to ten inches from the
   speaker.

3. When you begin to record, say into the mike what record
    setting you are using. For example, record: "I am re-
    cording at one-half full record level."

4. Record ten to fifteen seconds of material at normal con-
    versational loudness.

5. Change the record level setting to two-thirds full volume
    and record onto the tape what volume you are using.

6. Record ten to fifteen seconds of material at normal con-
    versational loudness as before.

7. Change the record level setting to three-fourths full
    volume and announce what setting you are using.

8. Record ten to fifteen seconds of material as before.

9. Rewind the tape to the beginning and set the playback
    volume at one-third full volume. Do not change this
    volume setting during the next two steps.

10. Play the tape and note which setting (if any) yields the
    best volume, that is, the volume that is most nearly like
    the original loudness, but without distortion.

11. Also note any distortions from aspirated consonants or
    from the hiss of fricatives. If there are any present,
    adjust the mike position.

12. If none of the settings gives satisfactory results, that
    is, sufficiently loud volume, bring the mike closer to
    the source and/or ask the person to speak somewhat louder
    (without straining). Then repeat the trial-run procedure.

Whatever record level setting you find most satisfactory, use
that setting when recording your master. Avoid *riding gain*
(manipulating the controls during record operations), unless the
loudness of the sound source begins to change significantly.
Also, be very careful when making your master recording that you
keep the mike distance and source loudness the same as they were
during the trial run.

In discussing proper volume, we have emphasized that it is as
important to avoid volume that is too low as it is to avoid volume that is too high. By keeping his volume out of both zones,
the recordist will achieve the best recording results. Unfortunately, the most common record level indicator, the VU meter,
is not as helpful in avoiding these zones as the recordist might
like. Because the needle bounces so erratically on nonprofessional VU meters, the indicator cannot tell the recordist precisely the upper limit of the safe recording zone, the point at
which volume becomes excessive. Neither do the meters specify
the lower limit of the safe zone, the point at which volume becomes too weak. For this reason, record level indicators on

home recorders are not considered the best guides in establishing the correct input level.

On the whole, the trial-run procedure outlined above is the most faithful method of arriving at satisfactory volume. The record level indicators, however, do have a function. They may serve to verify the volume chosen by the trial-run method. Proper volume will ordinarily cause the indicators to peak into the distort zone. If this happens, do not be alarmed. It is very likely that no distortion has actually occurred on the tape. In fact, it is probably a good sign that you have the correct record level setting.

TIP: In a nutshell, the lower the playback volume required to deliver good output, the better. If one-half full playback volume or more is needed, manipulate the interrelated variables to bring the record volume adjustment closer to one-third.

Time taken to make systematic trial runs is time well spent. The procedure requires no more than about two minutes.

MIKELESS RECORDING

Live, in-person sound is not the only source of material for recording. Phonograph records, AM, FM, and shortwave radio broadcasts, television shows, or even other tape recordings provide a wealth of good sounds.

By placing the recorder microphone in front of the radio, TV, or record player, any of these sources can be taped. The resulting sound, however, will not be the best quality possible. The mike will pick up external noise, and as the sound passes through the source instrument's mike and amplifier, the quality will be degraded at every point. The preferred practice, then, is to link the source instrument directly to the recorder with a patch cord. External noise can be eliminated, and several points of degrading can be circumvented.

Mikeless recording is used most often for dubbing selections from records and copying music broadcasts from an FM radio. These two common situations will be discussed here. In Chapter 7, the use of other communication devices as sources of recorded material will be considered, and a discussion of copying from tape recordings will be presented in detail in Chapter 8.

From Records to Tape

The activity of copying records onto tape carries with it a number of striking advantages from the standpoint of economy, convenience, quality, and flexibility. If you have a source of records, it is far less expensive to tape them than to buy the records yourself. Records deteriorate with use; magnetic record-ings do not. Records lose very high frequencies and about three decibels in signal level on the first playing. Deterioration continues with subsequent playings. If you are fortunate enough to have access to a turntable, you can also avoid the cost of expensive phonograph equipment.

From the point of view of weight and bulk, tape and a recorder are usually far more convenient than records and a phonograph for those going abroad. Depending on the speed, reel size, and number of tracks being used, one reel of tape can hold a number of record albums.

Recording from records has the potential of giving you better sound reproduction than you can get from almost any other sound source. If the sound is transferred from a relatively new record, the quality should be very good. In order to capture the full measure of quality available, some experts counsel that a taped copy should be made from the first playing of a record, or at least the second. If you must buy records, it is wise to tape the material and use the taped version in preference to the rec-ord, which should be stored for copying purposes only. Copying also allows you to put together on a length of tape just the selections and arrangement of material you want. This flexibility is particularly appealing when all numbers on a record are not equally desirable. The ability to edit the tape provides even greater flexibility.

To record from records, the turntable and recorder should be linked with a shielded patch cord. Alligator clips on one end of the cord can be attached to the speaker terminals of the rec-ord player. This connection ordinarily requires opening the record player housing, if no output jack is provided. Precau-tions should be taken against electrical shock. The plug on the other end of the patch cord is for the recorder input jack.

It is extremely important that the discs be as free as pos-sible of dirt and lint. Records should be thoroughly cleaned with a special cloth or brush before recording.

The actual recording should be preceded by a trial run. The output volume of the record player should be adjusted so that the sound is at a normal listening level. Then, use the trial-run procedure suggested above to find the proper input setting for the recorder. To initiate recording, the needle should be placed in the record groove and the turntable rotated until the sound begins. The disc should then be turned back a revolution or two and held while the turntable continues to rotate below.

When the tape recorder is put in record mode, the record should be released. By the time the sound begins, the record will have reached its proper speed, and no click will be present. At the end of the disc, the tape recorder input volume should be turned to zero to avoid the final click as the needle leaves the disc.

From FM to Tape

Someone has said that FM is the abbreviation for *free music*. This is certainly true. With a printed schedule of station offerings, the music enthusiast can build a large private collection of fine music in a short while. As with phonograph records, both monophonic and stereophonic (multiplex) recordings can be made. Instructions for connecting your recorder to an FM radio and tuner, shortwave radio, or television are ordinarily contained in the booklet accompanying your recorder.

A nice feature of recording FM broadcasts is that the volume and frequency of the program is automatically monitored and regulated at the transmitting station. This means that the recordist need not worry about his record level setting once he has determined it by the trial-run procedure. There will be no surprising peaks of sound nor failing volume. Furthermore, FM stations will usually have no program content outside 30-15,000 Hz.

The general recording techniques covered in this chapter should serve as a guide regardless of the taping task. However, depending on where recording takes place, these general techniques will be easier or more difficult to apply. They are easiest to apply when the language recordist can draw his subjects away from their normal setting and record off-location, where all suggested quality-control measures can be taken. The techniques are most difficult to apply when the recordist must capture language material found only on-location. The unique problems created by this setting are discussed in the following chapter.

7 Language Recording Techniques

The focus of Chapter 6 was on the ideal recording situation and on how to approximate it. For some purposes, the language recordist will be able to follow the recommendations closely in order to escape from those typical on-location characteristics which compromise recording quality. He will choose his off-location studio for its good acoustic features and exercise the necessary control over extraneous noise, his instruments, and his subjects to produce his recordings.[1]

In this chapter, we are concerned with the other purposes of the language recordist, those for which material can be recorded only on-location, that is, in the setting which is natural for such language behavior. This setting may be out-of-doors or it may be indoors, but it is always characterized by the recordist's lack of control over participants and external noise. Special techniques are called for in this situation.

On-location recording presents the recordist with the most severe test of his skill and resourcefulness. He must accommodate himself and his tools to situations and subjects much as he finds them with all their variety and unpredictability. While few on-location recordings are as easy to make as off-location recordings, there is less uncertainty when subjects are aware they are being recorded. Their cooperativeness adds an important measure of predictability and enhances the possibility of making good recordings. When, for a variety of reasons, a recordist feels he must record without the speaker's knowledge, difficulties are greatly multiplied. Knowing cooperation is absent, unpredictability is greater, and good recordings are much harder to achieve.

Covert recording methods are often felt necessary when the public presence of recording tools destroys the possibility of getting the target material on tape. Such is the problem of those who are interested in studying everyday speech--rapid, casual, unaffected conversation. The dilemma is that the effort to record such speech often destroys it. The only way to get unself-conscious speech on tape is to record it. Yet, overt recording produces self-conscious, noncasual speech. One answer to this dilemma is to use covert recording techniques.

Many students of language behavior face this dilemma. Linguists and sociolinguists who study the linguistic patterns of casual speech find that it changes into careful speech whenever it is observed in an overt way. Developmental psycholinguists who study child language acquisition by observing normal parent-child and child-child interaction discover that such normal interaction ceases or is modified with the appearance of recording instruments. Language teaching researchers working to identify the everyday verbal routines which learners must master if they are to move easily in a foreign language and culture soon find that such interaction becomes stilted and unnatural when openly recorded. These are just a few of the many researchers who are looking for ways to deal with the problem of observing language behavior which is altered by observation.

Sometimes it is not simply that recording tools are inadmissible in certain situations, but that strangers are. Researchers of nonstandard language varieties and dialectologists investigating local dialects find that subjects may switch dialects or even languages when speaking with a stranger who does not share the dialect or language being spoken. The problems faced by folklorists, anthropologists, and others are equally perplexing. The study of myths, legends, rituals, and oral history, for example, is made difficult when the recordist cannot even observe the activities of the groups engaging in such speech events. He may be barred from certain religious ceremonies. If the recordist is a male, certain female gatherings are off limits and vice versa. Again, one answer may be covert recording. In all such cases, however, the recordist must judge the propriety of making such recordings.[2]

As the illustrations suggest, certain on-location recording situations are difficult to handle. Yet, because the study of unedited speech in particular has become one of the growing edges of research in a number of fields, experimentation and ingenuity are needed to meet the challenge.

We will look at overt and covert on-location recording under three headings: recording face-to-face interaction when the recordist is a participant, recording face-to-face interaction when

the recordist is not a participant being either an observer or
completely absent from the scene, and recording language data
from communication systems.

FACE-TO-FACE: PARTICIPANT RECORDIST

Overt Methods

The on-location recordist, like the roving reporter, will
have to conduct interviews with subjects who are either sitting
or standing. If this aspect of the situation can be anticipated,
preparations most appropriate to each kind of interview can be
made.

Seated Interviews. Seated interviews most often take place
indoors, in a living room or an office, for example. Microphone placement must be a primary consideration. If phonetic
detail is required from the recording, a lavalier or lapel mike
is imperative for maximum mike-mouth proximity. Even if phonetic accuracy is not demanded, this mike arrangement is still
to be preferred in most cases. An external microphone on a
stand or one built into the tape recorder will be adequate in a
quiet setting if positioned within two feet of the subject. The
recordist should be aware, however, that his input volume will
be uneven as the interviewee shifts about in his seat.

By anticipating which mike arrangement will be used, the recordist can adjust the interviewer-interviewee distance to best
advantage. The farther the two parties sit from each other, the
louder each will naturally speak to the other. When the subject
does not wear the mike, the recordist should try to sit at a
comfortable but not close distance. Seating distances make
little difference when the mike is worn.

A good general rule to observe from the beginning to the end
of a recording session is this: The less attention one needs to
give to recording equipment the better. One way to avoid spend-
ing time with the recorder at the beginning is to make several
advance preparations. The recordist should practice setting up
his equipment quickly and quietly. Tape should be put on the
machine, and speed and input volume should be preset. Then, after locating the microphone, and while chatting with the subject,
the recordist can put the recorder in record mode and make final
adjustments in volume.

To avoid interruptions during the interview, the tape used
should be sufficiently long to last the entire session without
being turned over. When using a battery-operated recorder, the
same care should be taken with batteries to insure that they
will handle a continuous drain for the whole period. Even so,
extra tape and batteries should be in the equipment kit.

Ideally the tape recorder should be on the floor out of the subject's view but close to the recordist in case problems arise. However, little overt attention should be paid to the equipment. With hands and eyes free of the recorder, the recordist can keep the focus on the social situation. He can take notes, maintain visual contact with the speaker, and participate naturally in the interview with facial expressions, nods, and other indications of interest and appreciation. Prepared questions, too, will often help sustain the flow of the interview and achieve the objectives systematically.

TIP: If the recordist notices that the subject's voice becomes softer during the interview, there is a generally effective remedy. The recordist should speak somewhat more loudly than usual. Surprisingly, the subject will often unconsciously reciprocate.

The value of skillfully handled tools can be quickly undone if the recordist displays visible concern over the recording process. An overwrought appearance will have a decidedly detrimental effect on a recording session. It is easy to begin worrying about the noise that may be present, the battery charge, how much tape is left on a reel. It is important to remember that a pained look will not erase the uncontrollable noise just recorded. Noise is simply in the nature of on-location recording. As for other worries, many can be forestalled if preparations such as those mentioned above are used. If there is some chance that tape length or battery power will not last through the interview, calculate the time at which adjustments will be needed. If it is necessary to keep an eye on the time, take off your watch before the session and place it so that it can be checked unobtrusively. When the change-over time arrives, excuse yourself at an appropriate point and handle the matter quickly.

Standing Interviews. Standing interviews are conducted most often outdoors or in large indoor areas. Preparations for this situation are somewhat different from those needed for the seated subject.

As for equipment, a portable AC/DC machine is ordinarily used along with a microphone housing an electrical pause switch. A windscreen should be used as a matter of course, not just for gusty weather, but because the recordist creates wind across the mike face as he moves the mike from speaker to speaker.

The recordist will very likely have a mike in one hand and his recorder in the other. Under these circumstances, knob-juggling and even meter-monitoring will be very difficult and should not be attempted. In professional interviewing, a second person is often used to take care of the recorder to relieve the

interviewer. Without such help, the recordist should prepare
his recorder with adequate tape footage and battery power to
move nonstop through the interview. Well before coming face-to-
face with the subject, the recordist should preset speed and record level (if he is not using automatic volume control) and put
the recorder into record mode with the electrical pause off.
When the exchange begins, the mike switch can be flipped easily.

TIP: Tape should be new or bulk-erased. Otherwise, stopping
and starting the recorder, especially with an electrical
pause, may leave bits of unerased material between recorded
sections.

In his interview, the recordist should be able to move the
mike from speaker to speaker without having to look at the mike
directly. It takes practice to synchronize the movement with
the give and take of conversation while at the same time adjusting the mike for voice loudness and surrounding noise. If the
mike is thrust too quickly toward the subject, he will flinch or
back away; if it is too slow, the speaker's first words may be
faint. Smooth, regular movements are ideal. With practice, the
recordist should be able to handle his equipment so skillfully
that the casual observer will think recording is the easiest of
activities.

If it is not crucial for the recordist's voice to be heard
clearly, the microphone can be held continuously on the subject.
The closer the mike, the better, generally from five to eight
inches from the mouth. By maintaining this distance at about
chin level and slanting the microphone housing naturally toward
the speaker's mouth, good recordings can be achieved even in
relatively noisy surroundings. Working in conjunction with a
close mike technique is the fact that we tend to speak louder
outdoors than we do indoors at the same distance.

Certainly a vital part of all on-location recording is the
job of creating a receptive climate for whatever recording is to
be done. In our own culture, observance of courtesies will do
much to pave the way for a successful interview: Make appoint-
ments well in advance, confirm them shortly before the interview,
hold to time limits, express appreciation verbally and in writing, and so on.

In cross-cultural situations, establishing rapport is especially delicate, but it is vital in person-to-person contacts.
Of primary importance is the recordist's respect for local cus-
toms. This may require him to probe into the appropriate behavior expected of guests in interpersonal contact with a host.
Second, the recordist, as the guest, must offer a clear statement of who he is and why he comes, presented in terms of roles

the host is familiar with. This, too, may take some careful advance preparation. Little can be accomplished if the host doubts the veracity or motive of his guest. Third, the recordist should be sensitive to negative reaction to recording. His desire to record certain types of material from particular persons at certain times or places may be met with staunch resistance. Some personal or culture-bound reason, unknown to the recordist, may be behind such hesitation. Whatever the explanation, it must be respected. Another time, subject, approach, or situation may be necessary before the recordist can get the recording he wants.

Some individuals develop mike fright if they are unfamiliar with tape recorders. They may display nervousness and be at a loss for words even though ordinarily they may be quite talkative. It is the responsibility of the recordist to be alert to such signs and move to forestall or relieve the tension not only for the sake of the recording, but also for the sake of the host.

A sympathetic approach and several methods may be needed to draw attention away from the recording itself. First, prior to recording, it is often helpful to move into a topic slowly, giving the host a sufficient chance to get to know his guest. The businesslike attitude of getting right to the point is not universally understood or appreciated.

Second, if possible, the recordist should share with the host the kind of information that is sought. Such reciprocity on the part of the guest shows not only his genuine interest but also his willingness to give of himself in the situation. A sample of material from the guest also helps the host to see clearly what the guest is interested in.

Third, the use of a tape recorder can be explained in understandable terms. Its presence can stand as an admission of the recordist's limitations, if he says simply that he may not remember everything the host says. Such an admission, besides being true, has the positive effects of making the recordist human and of reducing suspicion.

Fourth, if it seems appropriate, an unobtrusive recording could be made of such interaction to eliminate certain barriers. Playback of casual conversation will often be amusing, but it may also lay to rest any apprehensions the host may have about the function of the recorder. A sample recording will also give the recordist an opportunity to check record level, mike distance, and so forth.

These various methods aim at easing the tensions that a recording session may produce, so that the social situation may be preserved and the recorded product may reflect as much as possible the natural flavor of the interaction.

Covert Methods

Standard interview techniques are often inappropriate and impractical for gathering casual speech material and for rapid and
anonymous interviews. The methods discussed here involve the
recordist and a subject who may be unaware of being recorded.
Because of constraints on how close to the subject's mouth a
concealed microphone can be placed, recording quality is not
equal to that achieved by the use of a lavalier microphone. However, with ingenuity and planning, acceptable quality can be
obtained.

Covert Microphone and Overt Recorder. In the standard interview, an overt mike and an overt recorder are used. With the
addition of a covert microphone, it is possible to record the
subject within the standard interview format without his being
aware of it. In this way, nonformal speech can be gleaned in a
formal situation.

The equipment needed is a cassette or open-reel recorder
which permits recording with an external microphone, but which
also has a built-in microphone. This is a characteristic of
most portable cassette recorders. Since the built-in is ordinarily marked by no more than a set of perforations in the recorder, it passes unnoticed to the casual glance, hence, the
covert mike. Especially convenient are machines which automatically continue recording, but with the built-in mike, when
the external mike is unplugged.

For this method, the recorder must be placed as close to the
subject as is convenient, for example, on a table beside the
subject's chair. A cover over the reels or cassette is important so that the tape noise or turning reels will not draw
attention to the machine.

Before the external microphone is set up, the recordist makes
mention that he should check to see that the tape is blank. Upon
playing a bit of the tape, he "discovers" what he has previously
prepared: a recording, preferably something short that the recordist and subject can laugh about. Explaining that his machine
works best when old material is first erased, the recordist puts
the recorder in record mode "to erase the tape." The recordist
and subject can then chat "while the tape is erasing." Since
the external mike is obviously not connected to the recorder, it
appears that the machine is not recording. It is recording, of
course, through the built-in microphone. If AVC is used, the
manual volume control can be turned to zero without affecting
the input volume, for the added impression of "erasing." After
a convenient time, the recordist can "check the tape," plug in
the external mike, and go on with the formal interview.

If the interview has formal segments in it, such as a questionaire or a reading passage, the recordist can initiate intermissions between the segments. The external microphone is unplugged from the recorder in a noticeable way while the machine is in record mode, austensibly to stop the recording. As before, recording continues through the built-in mike. It is often the case that interviews with tasks in them build up tension and strain on the subject. The break between segments capitalizes on this fact by providing a time to relax. Nonformal speech can be obtained during such breaks. The contrast of such speech with the adjacent formal segments of the interview can be striking. When the formal segments are resumed, the external mike is again plugged in.

Covert Microphone and Recorder. The methods suggested in this section require the recordist to wear a concealed microphone and inconspicuously carry or wear a small tape recorder as he interacts with his subjects. Because of their small size and weight, standard or pocket cassette recorders are most appropriate for this purpose.

Experience has shown that the recordist must wear the microphone high on his person, for example, under the collar, inside a tie, in a shirt pocket, or fastened under the clothing with no more than one layer of cloth over the mike face. The higher the mike, the closer it comes to the cospeaker's mouth, and the better the chance for a good recording. It has proven unsatisfactory to have the mike with the recorder in a box, bag, or briefcase which is carried under the arm or at the side. The input volume is generally too poor, and sounds from the machine are detrimental to an already poor recording.

Pencil or box-shaped microphones are often more difficult to conceal than button microphones. About the size of a large coat button, these mikes are available in all degrees of quality and price. Less expensive mikes generally have greater sensitivity, but lower and rougher frequency response than expensive mikes. This means that the former will put a higher sound level on the tape than the latter, all other factors being equal. This greater sensitivity can be used to offset greater speaker-mike distance to a slight degree, provided the loss of frequency response and smoothness is not crucial.

The microphone line runs under the clothing to the recorder. If the recordist carries the instrument, the mike line may lead to a briefcase, shopping bag, book bag, purse, box, shoulder bag, package wrapped for mailing, or other appropriate container. The advantage of carrying a tape recorder in a container is that the standard cassette machine can be accommodated regardless of its size along with other auxiliary equipment, to be discussed below.

A major consideration in choosing a container is ready accessibility to the recorder. The controls must be used; tape supply must be renewed by turning the cassettes over or inserting new ones; battery condition will be monitored periodically; and the recordist may need to attach or detach the microphone quickly, if the occasion arises. Arrangements which allow these matters to be taken care of easily and inconspicuously are preferred.

Before encountering one's subject, the recordist should place the machine in record mode. The machine begins recording and using tape from the moment the record button is depressed. If many short, closely sequenced interviews are to be done, it is useful to set up a pause switch which can be conveniently activated without having to open the container. In this way, tape consumption can be regulated as necessary. Instructions for making a pause switch are found in note 11 of Chapter 1. If longer, more spread-out interviews will be done, the switch, while convenient, is of less value since time will be available before and after each encounter to tend the controls.

TIP: Because most controls on cassette recorders are so sensitive to the touch, it is wise to tape down the record/play button with masking tape so as not to lose the record mode if the container is bumped.

For some purposes, the constraint imposed by having to hold a container continuously in one hand may be undesirable. For more freedom, the smaller pocket cassette recorders are light enough to be worn on a belt under one's jacket or in the pocket of a heavier coat. Especially convenient on pocket cassettes is a built-in electrical or mechanical (locking type) pause switch. A homemade pause switch will serve nicely. With the machine in record mode, the recordist can easily regulate tape movement. He simply reaches into his pocket or under his jacket as if to remove his handkerchief and flips the pause switch as required.

Noisy surroundings and the distance between mike and subject are key problems in covert recording. Some pointers along these lines may be helpful. The recordist can physically narrow the distance between himself and his subject. When standing with his subject, the recordist will naturally observe conventional distances. Greater distance is ordinarily required when participants are face-to-face than when shoulder-to-shoulder or at right angles to each other as when looking at some object. By planning the encounter carefully, the recordist can narrow the space between his mike and the cospeaker.

Another way to reduce the problem of distance is somewhat more elaborate. A miniature battery-operated amplifier can be added to the system. The microphone line goes to the amplifier, and the amplifier is connected by a patch cord to the recorder. The volume control on the amplifier is set and taped in place. In operation, the amplifier will magnify the recordist's voice, perhaps excessively, but the level of the cospeaker's voice will be considerably improved. Amplifiers can be bought or built inexpensively. However, they must be matched to the impedance of the mike and recorder in order to operate efficiently.

As with any recording, the quieter the setting the better. The recordist should avoid engaging a subject near or under a loudspeaker. The competition of announcements or background music in public places can destroy the intelligibility of taped material.

Covert Radio Microphone, Receiver, and Recorder. The system described here consists of three basic parts: a radio (wireless) microphone, radio receiver, and a tape recorder. The microphone is worn by the recordist, and the receiver and recorder are carried in a container much as described in the previous section. The difference is that no wires connect the microphone to other equipment. This feature leaves the recordist somewhat freer than when using the techniques already discussed.

There are in fact two sets of equipment which fit the description above. One is professional; the other, nonprofessional. The professional equipment will be described in the next section; the nonprofessional equipment is the subject of this section.

When the mike transmits signals, they are picked up by the radio and transferred directly to the recorder. The first component in this system is an FM radio microphone. It is a small battery-powered transmitter which has a broadcast range of about fifty feet under optimal conditions.[3] The second component is a common battery-operated FM radio. By tuning the mike manually to a vacant portion of the FM radio band, the recordist in effect creates a new FM station. The FM radio is connected to the third component, a battery-operated tape recorder. This connection can be effected by linking the radio to a portable tape recorder, open-reel or cassette, with a patch cord. No patch cord is needed when using the more compact and lighter radio-cassette unit offered by almost all makers of cassette recorders.[4]

Reception by the radio and transfer of signals to the recorder can be executed in absolute silence if the radio has an output jack which cuts off the speaker, as most radios do. The patch cord can lead from this jack to the recorder in one arrangement, or in the radio-cassette setup, the speaker can be cut off by a switch or by plugging an earphone into this jack.

As ideal as this system might appear, there are certain serious limitations which must be considered. First, the operating

range has been curtailed. At one time, this nonprofessional
system could operate at the remarkable distance of half a city
block. However, because of abuses to the system, in 1970 the
Federal Communications Commission instituted regulations which
restricted the effective range of transmitters. Now, when the
microphone is separated from the receiver by only a few feet,
the transmission is subject to severe fading because of interference from metal—cars, door frames, shelving, building materials, and so forth.

Second, while the microphone element may be any one of the
three major varieties, crystal, dynamic, or condenser, it transmits frequencies within the 50 Hz-5,000 Hz range only and must
be close to the sound source (within a few inches) to do so effectively.

Third, since the tuning device is generally not of high quality, the precise transmission frequency may wander slightly.
For this reason, it is best to use an FM radio with automatic
frequency control (AFC) which will lock onto the dominant frequency at a point on the FM band. In this way, the receiver
compensates for minor frequency shifts of the transmitter.

While the system is no longer as useful as it once was, it
can be used for what it does best: for transmitting at close
range, as between a mike worn on the recordist and a container
he may be carrying. A convenient feature can be added to the
system: an electrical pause control which is activated when the
bag or parcel is picked up or set down. The pause switch can be
mounted on the bottom of the container so that the weight of the
container against the floor will depress the button and start
tape movement. Lifting the container arrests movement. When
the system is in record mode, recording begins when the container
is put down, but stops when it is picked up again.

FACE-TO-FACE: NONPARTICIPANT RECORDIST

When the recordist cannot enter into the interaction from
which language data is desired, he may be able to get one of the
accepted participants to wear a microphone, overtly or covertly,
into the interaction. If this is possible, the methods suggested
above would come into play. Besides these methods, there are
several others that are available to the recordist.

Overt Methods

The connection between the mike and the recording equipment
is the principal consideration in the choice of methods. If
subjects are relatively stationary, mike lines can be accommodated; if subjects are moving around a great deal, the lines
will be inconvenient if not impossible.

Stationary Subjects. When indoor peer-group interaction is the object, the best sound quality will be attained by having each participant wear a lavalier or lapel mike. Each line goes to a mixer which combines the separate input lines into fewer output lines leading to a recorder. Alternatively, and preferably, each line can go directly to a separate channel in a tape recorder. A four-track stereo machine provides two channels; and an eight-track quadraphonic machine offers four simultaneous channels. Of course, more than one multitrack recorder can be used. Synchronization on playback is not difficult if the voice of at least one participant can be heard on more than one recorder.

TIP: Moving a mike plug from one jack to another can be accomplished in seconds; changing tape takes considerably longer. If the loss of recording must be held to a minimum when the tape runs out, it is best to have available an auxiliary machine already loaded with tape. Just before the original machine runs out of tape, the auxiliary recorder is put into record mode. The mike line plugs are moved rapidly from one machine to the other.

The participants may be seated or may move within a prescribed radius. If movement is anticipated, it is wise to anchor the mike lines securely to some part of the subjects' clothing, such as a belt, so that the pull of the lines will not dislodge the mikes. Also needed is sufficient mike line. The use of long lines prescribes the microphone impedance: Only low impedance mikes permit lines longer than about six feet.

The method suggested here assumes that the recordist is an observer and can handle the setup--mike placement, recorder monitoring, tape supply, etc.

Moving Subjects. When subjects are engaged in unrestricted movement, mike lines are out of the question. There are several kinds of equipment available which use no lines. They offer the recordist differing degrees of reproduction quality.

Television and movie studios use professional radio microphones to capture the sound of moving subjects. As outlined above, the system requires a battery-powered transmitter--the wireless microphone, a radio receiver, and a recorder. The professional equipment discussed here has notable advantages and disadvantages when compared with the nonprofessional system described earlier.

The advantages of the professional system lie in the quality of sound transmission and its effective range. The small microphone, worn on the subject, will supply the full audio range of

frequencies to the receiver for superb reproduction. Furthermore, it will do so at a considerable distance. The transmitter
can be separated from the receiving equipment by up to one-half
mile, although an operation range of no more than several hun-
dred feet is preferred.

The disadvantage of this system is that it is expensive.
There is the initial cost of transmitter and receiver which may
begin around $500. Multiple microphones require multiple re-
ceivers, all of which multiplies the cost. In addition, there
is the expense of a station license, since the transmitter may
be operated only on an assigned frequency outside the standard
FM band.

For certain applications, the advantages of long distance,
high quality transmission and superb portability characteristics
of the mike will outweigh the disadvantages. The language re-
searcher, in particular, should be aware of this option.

A second option is to record at a distance using either a
parabolic dish or a long-throw microphone. The characteristics
of these mikes are described in Chapter 3. The attractive feature of both mikes is that no equipment is worn on the informant.
The unattractive aspects, besides equipment cost, relate to
quality, portability, and maneuverability. The mikes operate
effectively only out-of-doors and ordinarily within 150 feet of
the sound source. The recordings made are unusable for an analysis of phonetic detail, although the content of conversation is
clearly intelligible as long as the subject faces the mike.
Neither system can be handled easily. Added to the bulk of a
microphone is the recorder and a tripod or similar facility for
steadying the microphone. As long as subjects do not move too
rapidly, the operator can keep his sight accurately on the sound
source. The constraints on portability and maneuverability of
the microphones restrict the use of this equipment to subjects
who move within relatively narrow confines.

Covert Methods

Subject-worn and large size microphones as described above
are used almost exclusively for overt recording purposes. When
a subject wears or carries a microphone, he does so ordinarily
being aware of its presence. Furthermore, unless preparations
are made to hide the instruments, bulky microphones and auxiliary
equipment are used in full view of the subject. For some purposes, conspicuous recording may be satisfactory; for other purposes, it may not. The latter interests can be served to a
greater or lesser degree by methods which involve planting a
microphone in the vicinity of the target sound.

Before attempting to gather recorded data with a planted microphone, the recordist must be certain that his goal is realis-
tically within the capability of a hidden recording device. It
is quite easy to make a recording in a room full of people talking. It is a considerably more difficult task to insure that
the recording captures the target material and that the material
will be intelligible and of sufficient quality to be useful.
The general noise level, participants moving to and from a mike
position, voices overlapping and masking each other all work
against good recording quality. For these reasons, mere proximity of mike to sound source is no guarantee that an adequate
recording can be made. Some recordings made close at hand turn
out poorly; others, made at a distance, can be quite satisfactory.
The following suggestions point to a realistic matching of recording goals and recording capability for indoor settings.

Circumstances may dictate where a microphone can be concealed
--whether close to or at a distance from the speaker(s). These
two general situations are examined in turn.

Recording Close Up. For best quality reproduction, a microphone installed for close-up recording should be located near a
focal point of activity--a desk, counter, lectern, playtoy--
where a minimum of background noise is present. It should be a
point at which only one or two individuals talk at a time and
where they talk for a sustained period of time. In a nursery
school, for example, a mike in, on, or by some object around
which one or two children gather will deliver usable material.
The competition of additional voices or other sounds--noise-
generating toys, music, hand clapping--will compromise the
quality.

The equipment to be used for close-up recording must be selected keeping in mind its concealability and control requirements: How well can it be hidden, and how much management does
it require?

The easiest equipment to conceal and control is the small,
self-contained and completely silent professional radio-micro-
phone. Once the mike is turned on, it transmits signals continuously. The recordist's management job is simple. After
putting a comfortable wireless distance between himself and the
mike, he can monitor all transmissions with his receiver and
record what he wishes.

The pocket cassette recorder, also self-contained when used
with its built-in microphone, can be hidden with relative ease.
It is especially useful when the target material can be captured
between the time the machine is put into record mode and the
time the tape runs out. If there is no automatic shutoff, the

recorder then quietly drains the battery supply until the recordist can retrieve his equipment.

TIP: For cassette recorders used in this way, the recordist
should prefer a machine with an automatic shutoff. Not only
does it save batteries--an incidental value, but it avoids
the inevitable motor wear and the potential for developing
a flat spot on the roller. However, the shutoff must
operate quietly or be so padded that its operation cannot
be heard.

An external microphone leading to a recorder of any type or
size presents special problems. While it is often possible to
place a small mike in an optimal position, the line and recorder
to which it is linked must also be kept out of sight. It is
ideal to locate the recorder outside the recording area. In
this situation, the recordist can comfortably use a larger recorder, even an open-reel machine with the extended recording
time open-reel tape affords. He can easily manage the recording
operation and need not be so concerned about recorder noises,
squealing tape, or flapping tape ends.

In situations where the recorder is on the scene with the
mike, the recordist must put the recorder in record mode in advance. From that point on, the critical problems are operation
noises and tape supply. AC/DC recorders are generally quieter
than AC-only models, and cassette tape is quieter than reel-to-
reel tape. While it may be possible to let the recorder run
continuously, especially with long-playing tape, it is often desirable to set the machine in motion at a specific time and cut
it off as necessary in order to regulate tape consumption. Although a remote control system could be built, two simpler means
of control are possible. One is to extend an electrical pause
switch to a place where the recordist can reach it. See note 11
in Chapter 1 on constructing a pause control. An even simpler
solution is to run the recorder on AC, using an outlet where the
recordist can plug in the power cord to begin recording and un-
plug it to stop recording.

Recording at a Distance. A recording made with the microphone more than ten feet from a speaker can be of satisfactory
quality if the subject is speaking in relatively quiet surroundings. An ordinary mike at a distance from the source will pick
up the sound more adequately if the speaker uses a public address system. Without such a system, some compensation is desirable, if not imperative. First, the microphone should be
mounted so that persons and objects will not obstruct the line-
of-sight path between speaker and mike. Ordinarily this will
mean installing the microphone above eye-level. Second, the
concealed microphone can be attached to a small amplifier which

boosts the signal received at the mike before it enters the recorder.

With the exception of the auxiliary amplifier, the equipment and control requirements for recording at a distance are similar to those mentioned in the previous section.

RECORDING FROM COMMUNICATION SYSTEMS

The least demanding recording situations involve recording language material from a communication device, such as a radio, television, or telephone. The recordist is one step removed from the actual face-to-face encounter, and thus can devote more attention to the recording process, and he may do so in the privacy of his own home. Because of the limiting conditions inherent in various communication systems, the best quality recording equipment will not be necessary.

Overt Methods

One-way broadcasts on AM, FM, and short-wave radio and on television all use licensed, public frequencies. The programs are recorded--often prerecorded before broadcast time--and participants are aware of it. Furthermore, any listener may record for his own private use anything on these frequencies. Thus, recording from radio or television is not a covert activity.

A voluminous quantity and variety of language material is available on these public media. It is readily transferred to tape by following the instructions in the recorder manual for a direct-line hookup. Trial-run procedures were outlined in Chapter 6. The recorded results can be quite good since radio and television transmissions use a wide portion of the audio range and are monitored to avoid peaks in volume. Thus, once a record setting is found, it can be used without modification for the entire broadcast. The same quality cannot be assured when the recordist must use a microphone juxtaposed to the speaker of the communication device. Along with the broadcast, any external noises in the vicinity will be picked up as well. Furthermore, by filtering the program material through a speaker and a microphone, the quality of the end product will be inferior to a direct-line recording.

Covert Methods

Two-way communication media are essentially for private interaction. In this category are telephone conversations, citizen band radio exchanges, and dispatcher-carrier communications as in taxicabs, delivery trucks, police cars. Although verbal interaction over any of these systems might be overheard, it is not ordinarily tape recorded. Several covert methods, however, make recording a simple matter.

Radio communications can be intercepted by means of a receiver tuned to the proper frequency. Some radios permit direct-line recording; others require the less satisfactory method of holding a microphone to the speaker. In either case, audio quality is generally poor because of the kinds of microphones used, the noisy point-of-origin environment, static and interference characteristic of these systems. Nevertheless, message content is discernable and thus useful for certain kinds of study.

Telephone conversations can be monitored and recorded by means of a line tap, an induction coil (telephone pickup) on the handset, or a microphone over the earpiece of the receiver.

Wire tapping is the term used for a direct-line recording from a telephone. Legal requirements on phone taps hold that the participants be aware that a recording is being made and that they be reminded of the fact throughout the conversation by an appropriate signal, usually a timed beep. Telephone companies want only their approved coupling and beep equipment to be used for phone taps, and they make this equipment available on a rental basis.

A quality nearly that of the wire tap, but without mechanical coupling, is attainable with the induction coil. This inexpensive telephone pickup device is attached by means of a suction cup to the plastic housing of the handset on the earpiece end. The coil converts vibrations from the handset into electricity. Since the voices of both parties cause the handset to vibrate, both voices can be picked up readily. These electrical pulses are sent along to the recorder over a two- or three-foot line.

One important factor in the recording quality attained is the impedance match between coil and recorder. If the two are badly mismatched, there may be only faint reproduction. If the mismatch is not so serious, there will be a background hum in the recording not present in the actual communication. Experimentation with different coils and different recorders is the best solution for this problem.

An ordinary microphone can be used as a third, but last-resort, method for recording telephone conversations. If your recorder allows you to monitor what you record as you record it, satisfactory recordings can be made. Masking tape can be used to fasten the mike face securely over the perforated disc of the earpiece. Hold the handset upside down with the earpiece down and the mouthpiece up. Speak into the mouthpiece holding it

closely to your lips. Listen to the person at the other end
through the recorder monitor system as you record the conversation.

If your recorder does not allow you to monitor as you record,
then you must be able to hear the conversation through the earpiece directly. If a desk phone is being used, the most convenient way to arrange the mike on the handset is to fasten the
mike with masking tape on one end so that its face is pointing
in the same direction as the earpiece points, namely, toward the
speaker's head. By holding the receiver loosely to the ear,
sufficient volume will reach the mike. However, since the record level is set high in order to pick up the incoming voice,
the recordist should remember not to speak overly loud when he
talks. To do so will produce distortion on the tape.

One point is worth emphasizing. Even under the best circumstances, telephone speech is not equivalent in quality to radio
or television broadcast speech. The telephone transmitter is a
carbon microphone in the mouthpiece of the handset. It is known
to be the poorest of all microphones. Ordinarily the mouthpiece
will not transmit signals with frequencies above 3,400 Hz. This
range is adequate for voice when content, not fine phonetic distinctions, is important. Unfortunately, not even a full 3,400 Hz
can reach the analyst's ear because of the frequency loss at
every transmitting and receiving point from the first transmission when the speaker speaks into the mouthpiece of the handset, to the last when the recording is played back through the
recorder speaker.

In this chapter, we have presented an array of options available to the language recordist who finds himself in a variety of
on-location settings and circumstances. Undoubtedly, a vivid
imagination and the exigencies of one's situation will create
other options and combinations of options. It has been our concern to help the recordist evaluate the options we have discussed for his particular needs and stimulate him to find other
options which will give him the best possible recording results.

8 Editing Techniques

It is very difficult to make a completely noise-free recording
that needs no alteration. Since most recordings for general use
ordinarily require some modification in order to be considered
finished products, editing is an important skill to develop.
Essentially, it involves changing the composition of a recording
by removing, adding in, or rearranging material.

Fortunately, recording tape and the signal on it are of such
a character that they permit editing. The thin tape backing can
be cut easily and repaired, as is done in splicing; the magnetically induced signal can be moved readily or copied, as is
done in erasure and dubbing.

These editing techniques, and the jobs they can do are indicated in Figure 11. From this matrix, it is evident that some
editing tasks can be handled by more than one method. However,
not all available methods are equally desirable for an editing
task nor equally suitable for open-reel and cassette tape. In
this chapter, we will evaluate the appropriateness of the various
techniques for different situations and discuss ways to combine
techniques to best advantage.

THE CHALLENGE OF AN INVISIBLE SIGNAL

The signal and noise on a tape are patterns of magnetism in
the oxide. Since the recording process does not change the
color of oxide particles, nor etch them, nor move them around,
there is no visible evidence that the patterns are present.
Yet, to edit--to remove a bit of noise, for example--we must
know precisely where the patterns are which are responsible for

the noise. The challenge fundamental to editing is to locate
the invisible patterns.

Method \ Purpose	Removing	Rearranging	Adding In
Erasure By Head	x		
By Pen	x		
Splicing	x	x	x
Dubbing	x	x	x

Fig. 11. Editing Purposes and Methods

Following the metaphor used earlier, if the function of the
playback head is to *read* the magnetic patterns on tape, then the
head must also be able to *see* them. This is, in fact, the way
we meet the challenge just mentioned. The playback head gap
must be our eyes temporarily. The playback head (the rightmost
head on machines which feed from left to right) reads off which-
ever patterns happen to be on that portion of the tape touching
the head gap. Thus, if we are looking for the beginning of some
noise, we know exactly where to find it: It will be opposite
the middle of the playback head the moment we hear it. Once located, however, the patterns are no more visible than before.
So, we must stop the tape at the precise moment we hear the
noise beginning and make a mark on the tape opposite the playback gap. After the visible edit spot marks are made, we can
depend more fully on our eyes to finish the editing task.

Locating and marking the edit spots, then, are two basic
operations which must be completed before we can add, remove, or
rearrange material on a tape. Because of their importance,
attention is given to each operation.

Locating the Edit Spots

Edit spots are points on the tape which the editor needs to
identify for his editing. Typically, they are boundary points:
the beginning and end of good material, the beginning and end
of some noise. The editor will find that boundary points bear

different relationships to each other and represent essentially
two situations.

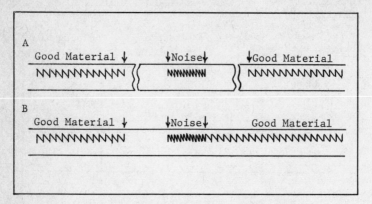

Fig. 12.   Two Editing Situations

In Figure 12, situation A, good material is one or more seconds from the material to be edited out.   (One second equals
7 1/2 inches at 7 1/2 ips, or 3 3/4 inches at 3 3/4 ips.)   Here
there are distinct, widely separated boundaries (↓) to be located and marked.   In situation B, the distances are greatly reduced.   To the left of the noise, good material is less than one
second away although still separated by some silence.   Editing
in these circumstances is referred to as *close editing*.   On the
right, good material is so close to the noise that a single
boundary mark will suffice for the end of good material and the
beginning of noise.   Editing at such a point will be called
ultraclose editing.   Playback speed of the tape is also an important variable.   Close boundaries at 3 3/4 ips will be ultraclose at 15/16 ips.

Situation A: Remote Boundaries.   In situation A, the boundaries of noise are far enough away from good material that they
can be found with little difficulty.   We let the recorder move
the tape at *one speed slower than normal.*   When we hear the beginning or end of the noise or signal, we quickly stop the tape
with the mechanical pause or stop button and mark the spot.   We
will overshoot the boundary slightly with this method, but it is
easy to place the marks so as to compensate for this error.

To determine carefully the amount of compensation to provide,
the editor may want to compare the mark made at the head using
the recorder-fed technique just described with the mark made by
the hand-fed technique outlined below.   The difference between
the two marks is the approximate distance in tape by which he

will generally overshoot the boundary. If one slower speed is not available, the editor must use either the normal playing speed with which overshooting will be greater or the technique described under situation B below.

If the noise is sufficiently distant from good material, it is enough to mark only the beginning and end of the noise. This is important for splicing. However, if we are using the edit pen or erase head method, even these marks are unnecessary as long as the general area of noise is known.

When editing cassette tape, situation A can be accommodated fairly well. Although the cassette recorder speed cannot be slowed down, 1 7/8 ips is slow enough that quick reflexes can stop the tape very close to the target boundaries. A more accurate, but more involved, way of locating boundaries is described in the following section.

Situation B: Close and Ultraclose Boundaries. The boundaries in situation B must be carefully identified because of the likelihood of making an editing error. For this reason, we must find the boundaries by moving the tape *by hand* across the playback head. This procedure is available for both open-reel and cassette tape editing.

For open-reel tape, we should remove the tape from between the capstan and the rubber roller after stopping at the approximate edit spot. With the tape still opposite the heads, we let the tape ride on the far side (not the rubber-roller side) of the capstan, as shown in Figure 13. In this way the capstan will not pull the tape along. The recorder should be put into playback mode letting the pressure pads and tape guides hold the tape in place. We then move the tape manually back and forth across the playback head until the exact spot is found. On some machines, this method is used more easily because the mechanical pause control can be locked while in playback mode to separate the capstan and roller. The reels can then be moved manually without removing the tape from its normal position.

Locating ultraclose boundaries is imperative for ultraclose head erasing and splicing. While these two editing techniques are used most readily on open-reel tape, they are not off-limits for cassette tape, given some editing gymnastics. Although we do not recommend these procedures for most editing jobs, the editor should be aware of them for his occasional need.

The gymnastics required involve playing a cassette tape on an open-reel recorder. To begin with, the editor pulls the tape out of the case at the head portal and runs it around the tape guides of the open-reel recorder, past the heads, but not between

the capstan and roller, as shown in Figure 13. A half twist in
the tape is necessary to put the oxide coating against the heads.
Manual feeding is now possible. By holding the tape on either
side of the tape slot, the editor can position the tape so that
it will contact the playback head.

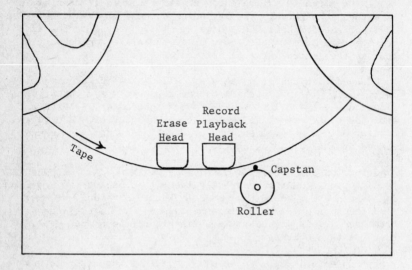

Fig. 13. Tape Path for Manual Playback

It is also possible to play the cassette tape on an open-reel
recorder at the normal 1 7/8 ips speed or at 15/16 ips (for locating situation A boundaries). The spindles on open-reel recorders are precisely the same diameter as the hole in a cassette hub. Furthermore, the fit is tight enough so that no
flanges on the spindle are needed to hold the hub in place. The
editor's first step, then, is to place the cassette take-up reel
over the open-reel take-up spindle. Then he routes the tape as
described above, passing it between the capstan and roller, and
giving it the necessary twist. After slipping a small diameter
stick under the tape close to the heads to hold the tape up to
the playback gap, the editor can play the cassette.

Certain cautions are in order. First, the editor should
handle the tape very carefully. Second, he should not touch the
tape or he will find he has produced massive signal dropout
where fingerprints have been left on the coating. To avoid this,
the editor can use film editor's gloves or he can simply put a
bit of double-faced cellophane tape on thumb and forefinger and
make a pad on the cellophane with a small circle of cloth.
Third, the editor should not use fast forward or reverse to wind

the cassette tape. The tape will stretch and snap, or the leader will break loose from the hub when the tape reaches the end.

It takes a little practice to become familiar with the sound of a recording being played as you pull it along. However, given such practice, the boundaries of the smallest segment of recording can be marked with absolute accuracy.

Marking the Edit Spots

The construction of different tape recorders makes it easier or more difficult to mark the edit spots directly. When using an open-reel tape recorder, the head cover should be removed to expose the heads. Ordinarily, this allows the editor to make his marks directly on the tape opposite the playback gap. On some machines, however, the head cover cannot be removed easily, or after removing it, the heads cannot be reached with a marking tool. In such cases, marking is done in two stages. First, when the exact location on the tape is found, the editor marks the tape at a premeasured point to the right of the head, say three inches from the playback head gap. Second, after removing the tape from the tape slot, the editor measures three inches to the left of his mark and makes a second mark. The second mark corresponds to the point on the tape opposite the head gap. To facilitate measuring in stage two, some editors fasten a piece of a ruler onto a handy surface of the recorder.

A china marker or preferably a finely pointed permanent ink marker may be used for writing on the tape. On open-reel tape, the marks should be placed on the tape *backing* only. Since the waxy substance of china markers comes off onto the pressure pads and tends to cause tape layers to stick together, the marks should be cleaned off the backing when editing is completed.

Since boundary marks can look very much alike to the editor when he begins to apply some editing technique, it is helpful to identify the kind of boundary being marked. Is it the boundary of noise or of signal? Is it the beginning or the end? Marks of different colors and/or shapes will facilitate editing considerably. Special guidelines applicable when splicing are mentioned in the section on splicing below.

Marking cassette tape is especially problematic. First, the tape cartridge must be removed from the machine. Then, since the coating side of the tape is exposed through the head portal, only the tiniest mark should be made on this side. No marking problems arise when the cassette tape is being used on an open-reel recorder. In either case, a permanent ink marker should be used, not a china marker.

Having faced the challenge of locating the invisible magnetic patterns for editing, we can turn now to the editing techniques themselves. In the discussion of each technique, there is an evaluation of its strong and weak points summarized in the TIPS. In the final section of this chapter, we show how the strengths of different techniques in combination can offset some of their weaknesses.

EDITING BY ERASURE

The erasure technique removes the recorded signal by changing the magnetic patterning of oxide particles. This change can be brought about by using either the recorder erase head or a permanent magnet.

Erase Head

There are two ways to use the erase head to remove unwanted material. In one method, the recorder pulls the tape along; in the other, the editor feeds the tape manually past the erase head. Each method has its own special uses and drawbacks.

Recorder-Fed Erasing. To erase by means of the erase head while the tape is in the tape slot as usual, the recorder is placed in record mode and the input volume control turned to zero. In this way, the erase head cleans the tape for new signal, but the zero setting prevents new signal from being recorded.

For some machines, the zero setting does not silence the record head entirely. Some recorders put a click on the tape when the recorder is put into and taken out of record mode. There are several solutions available for this problem. One involves removing the clicks; others avoid the clicks. The solutions are principally for open-reel tape.

If the editor is using an open-reel machine with a mechanical pause control, he can remove some of the clicks easily. With the pause on, he puts the machine in record mode. Then, turning the tape reels by hand to pull the tape to the left a few inches, the editor positions the click to the left of the erase head. When the pause is released, the erase head removes the click as it passes by. This maneuver takes care of initial record-mode clicks and those incurred in the middle of a recording. However, left remaining is the click produced as the machine leaves record mode.

The initial record-mode click can be avoided at the beginning of an open-reel or cassette tape if the leader lies opposite the record head at the moment the record mode is activated. The pop will not be recorded on the uncoated leader. Mode change clicks which occur within the tape or at the end, however, cannot be avoided by use of leader.

A technique for avoiding initial, medial, and final record mode clicks on open-reel tape is to insert a plastic shim between the tape and record head gap before entering or leaving record mode. The shim need be no more than the plastic pocket clip on a removable ballpoint pen top. Inserting the shim is perhaps a bit easier when a mechanical pause is first used, but it can be done readily without the pause. Under no circumstances should the electrical pause control be used in editing, since it creates a pop itself.

When erasing, the editor will know his starting point, but it may be difficult for him to see the stopping point if it is signaled only by a mark on the tape backing. For this reason, he may want to affix a tab on the open-reel tape at the final boundary or use the index counter for either open-reel or cassette tape.

Positive and negative features of this way of editing are given in the TIPS below:

PROS: (1) This method is best suited for erasing long sections of tape. (If an entire reel of tape is to be erased, use the bulk eraser, not the erase head.) (2) It is equally available for open-reel and cassette tape. (3) Since it erases the tape track by track, one track can be erased leaving adjacent tracks untouched. (4) By affecting only the signal, the tape backing is not weakened as it is when splicing. (5) The method provides a cleaner erasure than a permanent magnet, although neither are as clean as a bulk eraser. (6) Erasure can be done at the fastest tape speed available on the recorder regardless of the playing speed of the material to be erased.

CONS: (1) Without precautionary measures, electromagnetic erasure usually leaves a click on the tape when entering and leaving record mode. Since the measures are not fully available when using a cassette recorder to erase, all the clicks cannot be avoided. (2) The movement of the tape by the transport system makes this method unsatisfactory for very small removal jobs, such as a cough or a pop. (3) When the material has been erased, a space of silence is left on the tape. This may be undesirable in some places. (4) Head erasing cannot fade sound in or out of a recording.

Hand-Fed Erasing. For the closest possible removal tasks, even when *no* silence exists between noise and good material, the

hand-fed method of erasing is excellent. As in recorder-fed
erasing, the erase head is activated by putting the recorder in
record mode. Unlike the above technique, three requirements
must be met for the success of this method. First, the editor
must have clear visual access to the erase head. Second, the
tape must not be pinched between the capstan and roller, in order to use hand feeding. Third, the tape must not touch the
record head gap, in order to avoid all magnetic interference.

The first prerequisite immediately excludes the use of cassette recorders for this type of editing. However, single-track
cassette tape can be erased manually on an open-reel recorder as
described above. The second prerequisite can be met easily by
removing the tape from between the capstan and rubber roller as
illustrated in Figure 13. One way of meeting the third prerequisite to keep the tape away from the record head is to place
a plastic cover over this head. Another way is to route the
tape as shown in Figure 14.

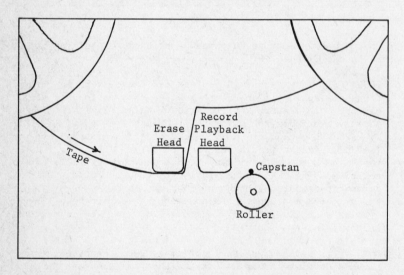

Fig. 14. Tape Path for Manual Erasing

Letting his boundary marks guide him, the editor manually
moves the tape past the erase head, carefully exposing the noise
on the track to the head gap. The gap is so fine that erasures
can be made as close to good material as the editor can confi-
dently move the tape. When the erasing has been completed, the
editor changes to playback mode in order to check his erasures.

The strength of this technique lies in its potential accuracy
for close and ultraclose editing. The editor can readily

accommodate the editing demands made by situation B, Figure 12.
He can take care of situation A even more easily, especially
when the noise to be erased is short. In fact, if the noise
boundaries are at least six inches from good material, the editor may not need to mark the boundaries before erasing. Guidance
from the index counter will be sufficient.

Regardless of the editing task, there is one caution the editor must observe when handling tape with material on adjacent
tracks. While editing on track 1, he will erase part of track 2
(and 3 and 4, if present) if he removes the tape from the tape
slot by lifting it past the activated erase head. The safest
procedure is to change modes before removing the tape.

The assets and liabilities of this technique are listed in
the following TIPS:

PROS: (1) This method is ideal for all close and ultraclose
removal jobs. (2) It is best suited for dealing with short
sections. (3) No clicks are left on the tape when entering
or leaving record mode. (4) On open-reel tape, one-track
editing is possible without disturbing adjacent tracks.
(5) The tape backing is not weakened. (6) A more silent
erasure is gained with the erase head than with the permanent
magnet edit pen.

CONS: (1) This method is not for editing multitrack cassette
recordings. (2) A silent gap is left after erasing. (3) The
erase head cannot be manipulated to produce fading effects.

Permanent Magnet Edit Pen

Any permanent magnet can be used to provide tape erasure.
Wherever the magnet is touched to the oxide coating of the tape,
the magnetic patterning will be altered. Therefore, the smaller
the magnet pole used, the smaller the area that can be erased
without affecting other signals. A convenient way to manage a
small magnet is to attach it to a handle of some kind. For ease
of reference we will call this tool an *edit pen*.

An edit pen can be made easily. Use an Alnico magnet approximately 1/4 x 1/4 x 1 inch. This type of magnet has a stronger
and longer lasting magnetism than other common magnets. It can
be bought at any hardware store for a few cents. Heat one end
of the magnet and embed it one-fourth inch into the end of an
empty plastic shaft of a ballpoint pen.

To effect the best erasure, the strongest part of the edit
pen should be passed precisely over the magnetically printed
material. The cleanest erasure, therefore, will be achieved by

lightly touching the *point* of the edit pen to that portion of
the tape *coating* where the track being erased is located.

How the editor uses this erasing technique depends on how
close good material is to the material being erased. Situations
A and B shown in Figure 12 are handled in different ways.

For situation A, the pen may be used while the tape is on the
machine. This particular approach cannot be used on cassette
recorders because of their construction. Using an open-reel recorder, the editor should hold the edit pen to the right of the
playback head while prepared to touch the oxide coating. As the
recorder plays the tape at one speed slower than normal, he can
apply the pen to the tape at the first boundary mark of the
noise and remove the pen at the second mark. Alternatively,
when the noise is far from good material, the editor need not
mark the edit spots at all. He can let the playback head guide
him. Putting the recorder in playback mode, the editor simply
applies the pen to the tape when he hears the noise at the playback head. He removes the pen as soon as he hears good material.
When the tape is played at one speed slower than normal, there
is ordinarily adequate distance between the playback head and
the editor's pen to complete these movements. Throughout the
editing process, care should be taken not to touch the pen to
the head or to the capstan, as it can magnetize recorder parts
on contact.

For situation B, the edit pen should be used only for close
editing, that is, when some silent space lies between the noise
and good material. Other techniques are preferred for ultraclose editing. The magnetic field of the pen is not sufficiently
focused to edit out noise which is nearly touching good material
without erasing some of the good material in the process. For
close editing of open-reel tape, the tape should be removed from
the tape slot after the boundary marks are made. It should be
laid, oxide up, on a smooth surface. The edit pen can then be
passed evenly along the tape between the marks.

With some dexterity, it is possible to apply the edit pen to
cassette tape off the machine. After the boundary marks have
been made, the cassette cartridge must be secured so that the
editor can use both hands for editing. A convenient way of
holding the cassette firmly is to clamp it carefully in a small
vise. A vacuum-base vise is handy for table-top work. Then,
with one hand, the editor holds the edit pen to the tape through
the playback head portal. With the other hand, he rotates the
hub of one reel using a slightly oversized pencil.

To produce the effect of gradually fading the sound in or
out, the magnet should be brought slowly toward the tape or

moved slowly away from the tape while moving along its length. The effect can be achieved on or off of an open-reel recorder and off of a cassette recorder.

An evaluation of the edit pen is given in the following TIPS:

PROS: (1) This method can be used more quickly than either erase head technique. (2) While being used most easily with open-reel tape, the edit pen can be used off the machine for removing noises from cassette tape. (3) It does not weaken the tape. (4) It leaves no click when applied or removed. (5) Erasing done on the machine may be done at the fastest tape speed available, although one speed setting slower than normal is preferred when good material is in the immediate vicinity. (6) The magnet can also be used to make the sound appear to fade in or fade out.

CONS: This method can be used when only one track has been recorded on the tape; it will destroy material on adjacent tracks. (2) It is not as practical as the erase head for long sections. (3) It is not as accurate as the erase head for ultraclose editing. (4) The erasure is not as silent as is possible with the erase head. The low hiss left by the pen is especially noticeable when program material has been recorded at low volume.[1] (5) It leaves a gap of silence.

EDITING BY SPLICING

The splicing technique affects the recorded signal by physically altering the tape on which the signal is recorded. To remove taped material, the section is cut out of the reel of tape and the gap closed and mended. Rearrangement can be accomplished by physically reordering tape sections then linking them together again. Material can be added in by cutting the tape at the place where the new material is to be introduced, adding the new section, then repairing the cuts. In addition to these editing purposes, the splicing technique is also used for repairing broken tape.

The tools needed in splicing can be very simple indeed: a cutting device and some mending material. The cutting device can be an ordinary pair of demagnetized scissors. Since magnetized scissors will leave a pop on the tape, it is wise to pass a head demagnetizer over the scissors before using them for editing. Devices more elaborate than scissors are also available. Many professionals prefer to use the block and blade method. The splicing block is a piece of metal (preferably not plastic) with a channel for the recording tape and a groove to guide the razor blade. An even easier apparatus to use is the splicer, looking somewhat like a desk stapler, which is a block

with a built-in set of blades and tape clamps. For occasional
use, the splicer is convenient. However, prolonged use tends to
throw the splicer out of adjustment, and worn blades and splicing pads sometimes are difficult to replace.

The mending material must be a tape especially designed for
splicing purposes. The adhesive on splicing tape is thinner,
lasts longer, and oozes less than the adhesive on common cellophane tape. When the gum gets on the recorder heads, the gummy
ooze will be detrimental to good recording and playback. It
also can cause uneven tape movement if tape layers are stuck together with the excessive adhesive.

   TIP: Never use any adhesive other than splicing tape for
   splicing. Major gumming problems thereby will be obviated.

Before your tools can be put to work, the splicing location
must be determined and marked accurately. Some pointers in
addition to the discussion provided above may be helpful. First,
it is far easier to edit a tape recorded at 7 1/2 ips or 3 3/4
ips than a tape made at 1 7/8 ips or 15/16 ips. The reason is
that the sound is spread over more inches of tape at faster
speeds than at slower speeds. Thus, it is easier to remove an
uh covering five inches of a 7 1/2 ips tape than to excise the
uh from a fraction of an inch of tape recorded at 15/16 ips.
This very difficulty is one source of frustration when trying to
edit cassette tapes recorded at 1 7/8 ips. If editing is
planned, consider which playing speed will permit you to do the
best editing job.

   Second, if the purpose of editing is to rearrange tape segments, number each segment according to its place in the new
sequence before cutting it out of the tape. Indicate which tape
edge is up by putting the boundary marks only on the upper half
of the tape backing. When the segments are cut out, they should
be rearranged by the numbers written on them. All marks should
be on the same half of the tape before splicing to avoid splicing segments in upside down.

   When the tape has been marked for cutting, the splicing process can begin. By following the procedures and cautions listed
below, perfect, long-lasting splices can be made every time.
Some good splices will last ten years or longer before the gum
dries out, or the tape gets brittle, and the splice comes apart.
Poor splices do not have so long a life.

   There are certain guidelines which apply to splicing and
which must be observed closely in order to produce good splices.
Three characteristics of poor splices should be avoided at all
costs: peeling, popping, and gumming. Peeling occurs when the

tape ends spliced together peel away from the splicing tape.
Popping is an audible noise heard as the splice passes the playback head. Good splices are never heard. Gumming occurs when
splicing tape adhesive is exposed to and rubs off on the recorder
heads.

1. The two tape ends to be spliced together should be overlapped (one-fourth inch or more) before cutting. The cut
   should cross the overlapped ends at a forty-five-degree
   angle to the tape edge. The surplus tape should be removed.

   Too shallow a cut will produce peeling.

   Too perpendicular a cut will produce popping.

   Note: If a broken tape is being mended at a point where
   recorded signal is present, step one should be skipped
   to avoid losing good material, unless the tape ends are
   badly stretched.

2. The tape ends should be butted together *shiny side* (backing) up before applying the splicing tape.

   Overlapped ends will produce popping and peeling.

   Ends which do not meet, but allow a space for splicing
   tape adhesive to be exposed to the heads, produce
   gumming.

3. The splicing tape should be placed over the ends and the
   excess tape trimmed by making a slightly concave cut into
   the tape on either side.

   No trimming or poor trimming exposes gum to the heads
   and produces gumming.

4. Air bubbles between the splicing tape and the recording
   tape should be rubbed out with your fingernail or with
   another smooth, hard object.

   Air bubbles, places where the splicing tape is not
   adhering to the backing, eventually result in peeling.

When the editor makes his splices, he should check his work
as he goes along. The angle of his cut and the presence of air
bubbles are readily visible. Overlapped tape ends and exposed
gum are nearly as easy to identify. If, after rubbing out all
the air bubbles, there remains a hair-thin bubble running parallel to the splicing cut, the tape ends have been overlapped. By
holding the splice up to a light with the backing toward the
light, any exposed gum will be visible either as a light streak
along the cut or as bits of splicing tape along the edges.

Air bubbles can be rubbed out and excess splicing tape along
the edges can be trimmed. But to correct the problem of a

poorly angled cut, overlapped tape ends, or ends which do not
meet, the splicing tape must be removed. The backing should be
peeled from the splicing tape beginning in the middle of the
splice at the cut.

When the editor finds he has made a splicing cut in the wrong
place, perhaps cutting into good material, the above procedure
should be used to correct the error. The splice should be taken
apart as described and the tape pieces .joined together as they
were originally. A new cut can then be made.

A great number of cuts can be made in a space as small as one
inch without affecting the sound, as long as there is no buildup of splicing tape. If a cut must be made into an area where
splicing tape covers the recording tape, the splicing tape should
be stripped before the cut is made. The pieces of recording
tape should be bumped together properly before applying more
splicing tape.

While these procedures apply equally well for open-reel and
cassette tape, splicing is not recommended for cassettes except
for repairs. A number of serious difficulties have been experienced when trying to edit cassette tape by splicing. First,
boundary marks for close and ultraclose editing can be made by
hand feeding the tape, but only with some difficulty. Second,
while the tape can be pulled easily out of the case with a
toothpick, the ultrathin tape is difficult to handle once it is
out. Third, the tape should not be touched with the bare hands.
Any moisture, oil, or dust on the tape will cause severe dropout.
Fourth, although the tape can be cut easily enough, it cannot
always be repaired satisfactorily. Ordinary splicing tape is
too thick to be used on the cassette tape. It will create a
bump in the winding and may cause poor winding and feeding.
Fifth, even when cassette mending tape is used, even the
slightest bit of exposed gum or unevenly abutted tape ends may
cause the tape to bind or jam. Sixth, splices on cassette tape
receive an extra amount of wear and therefore tend to peel, expose their gum, and come apart more often than splices on open-
reel tape. The reason for the extra wear is that cassettes use
a B wind which exposes the backing of the tape, and thus the
splice, to all the contact points in the case. For these reasons, other ways of editing cassette tape should be explored before turning to the splicing block.

Occasionally a cassette tape containing valuable material
does break. The editor must open the cassette housing in order
to retrieve the tape ends. This may be done easily if the case
is secured with screws. If the case halves are welded together,
as most are, they must be broken apart. A screwdriver carefully
inserted at the seam and twisted will open the case. After

splicing the tape ends together, the tape should be transferred to an empty, screw-fastened case which can be purchased for such purposes. The best step to take immediately is to copy the valuable material onto a new tape and throw the repaired tape away.

Positive and negative features associated with editing by splicing are presented in the following TIPS:

PROS: (1) Splicing is available for all editing tasks: adding, removing, and rearranging. (2) It is superb for ultra-close editing. (3) It is equally well suited to very large jobs. (4) There is no loss of recorded quality when splicing, as there is when dubbing. (5) No gap is left in removal operations. (6) Pauses of any length can be introduced as desired by using leader tape or blank tape. Appendix 5 presents a handy way to adjust tape length or time in order to add or subtract silence. (7) If the splice is well made, no click will be present.

CONS: (1) Splicing is usable only on one-track tapes. (2) While available for cassette editing, the technique is not recommended. (3) The tape backing is permanently weakened at the splicing point. (4) Although this is a most versatile method, it is also very time consuming.

EDITING BY DUBBING

The dubbing technique, like the erasure method of editing, affects only the recorded signal. But unlike the erasure methods, dubbing can be used to rearrange and add in as well as remove material. The objectives are accomplished by either transferring or not transferring signal from the recording (the original or master) to another tape (the dub, slave, or copy).

To dub, two machines must be linked with a patch cord from the output jack of the feed machine (containing the master) to the input of the receive machine (containing the blank tape). Although the most popular use of dubbing is to transfer the entire master to the blank tape without any alterations, various editing tasks can be handled easily. To avoid having certain material on the dub, that material is simply not transferred from the feed machine to the receive machine--removal by omission. To rearrange portions of signal, these portions need only be transferred to the copy in the desired order. To add in material, other tapes can be put on the feed machine and portions transferred to the dub as desired. To add in silence, the feed machine is stopped, allowing the receive machine to wind the required amount of tape onto its take-up reel.

Quality Control Factors

   As can be seen, dubbing is a highly versatile editing technique. Unfortunately, this is also the technique in which loss
of recording quality occurs. While the dub will never be equal
to the original, there are certain precautions which can be used
to hold the loss to an absolute minimum. By observing these
precautions and by beginning with a good quality master, it is
possible to produce a copy which is almost indistinguishable in
quality from the original. The key to successful dubbing lies
in understanding clearly the factors which enter into quality
control. The major factors are considered in this section.

   The *machines used* must have the same impedance rating, either
both high or both low, or else be appropriately matched. Unmatched recorders will affect the dubbing operation to varying
degrees. It simply may be impossible to transfer signal from
one machine to the other, or it may require an extremely high
feed-machine volume to get the most meager signal at the receive
machine. The signal may come through but be distorted or filled
with excessive static or hum. A copy made under these circumstances will be practically worthless.

   When two machines do not have matched impedances, it is pre-
ferable to try to find other recorders which do match. It is
possible, however, to have an impedance-matching transformer
made which will allow machines of differing impedances to be
used together. When recording between two matched high impedance machines, a shielded cable should be used to prevent the
cable from picking up hum from surrounding electrical fields or
from the ground.

   The heads, capstans, and tape guides of both machines should
be thoroughly cleaned and demagnetized before dubbing. The
pressure pads should be checked and cleaned if necessary. Such
precautions will tend to reduce any deviations in tape movement
which would contribute to wow and flutter.

   Head alignment will affect copying if the original recording,
made on a recorder with misaligned heads, is being played on a
recorder with properly aligned heads, or vice versa. Both
volume and high frequencies will be lost in the transfer process.
Less degrading will occur if the original recording is fed from
the same machine on which it was made, or, when a different feed
machine is at fault, if the heads are realigned.

   Wow and flutter is an especially problematic phenomenon when
duplicating tapes. The distortion tends to increase precipi-
tously because the wow and flutter from the feed machine, the
original tape, and the receive machine combine in the copy.

Such magnification of wow and flutter will become audible and disturbing unless the copying is done at very fast speeds--the faster the better. Fortunately, the dubbing speed does not have to be the same as the speed at which the original recording was made. Signal transfer occurs instantaneously. In commercial operations, dubbing may be done at 30 ips, 60 ips, or even 120 ips.

With nonprofessional equipment, such fast speeds cannot be attained, but often some increase is possible, and if possible, should be used. The simple scheme outlined below under dubbing speeds and the table in Appendix 6 will help you determine the fastest speed settings for the two dubbing machines in order to yield a copy of a given speed.

While extraneous noise will not affect the dubbing operation, *internal noise* will. In Chapter 6, we identified several sources of internal noise. One is the noise from the electrical functioning of the recorder, measured as the signal-to-noise ratio. Another source of noise is the transition from record mode to playback mode or vice versa. Other electrical disturbances constitute a third area for concern. Each of these sources will be considered briefly.

Tape recorder hiss inevitably increases from master to copy. Although there is nothing that can eliminate it, hiss can be offset by using a master recorded with proper volume, by using proper volume when dubbing, and by dubbing at the fastest speed possible. Since the receive machine is the one put into record mode, clicks will be left on the dub unless steps are taken to keep them off. While little can be done for cassette receive machines other than to begin recording on the leader, no clicks at all need appear on open-reel copies. To avoid record mode clicks, the procedures outlined earlier in this chapter under recorder-fed head erasing are equally applicable at the beginning, in the middle, and at the end of the dubbing process. One other source of internal noise is poor patch cords. Every weak connection is a source of static. The soldering of wires to plug terminals should be checked before using the patch cords.

The *frequency response* represented in the original will not be transferred intact to the copy. Some loss will be incurred. However, loss can be held to a minimum if the conditions mentioned in the preceding paragraphs are met, and if the playing speed of the dub is not slower than the playing speed of the original. If it is slower, the copy will have quality inferior to the original on the basis of the slower speed alone.

Dubbing Speeds

   The importance of using the fastest dubbing speed and of producing a copy with the proper playback speed has been emphasized.
In order to meet these dubbing demands, the editor must manage
three different speeds correctly: tape speeds, dubbing speeds,
and recorder speeds. The plural--speeds--is used to indicate
that for each speed there are at least two points at which that
speed is relevant. Tape speeds refer to the playing speed of
the master tape and the desired playing speed of the copy. Dubbing speeds deal with the speed setting used for the feed machine and the speed setting used for the receive machine. Recorder speeds have to do with the speed settings available on
the two dubbing recorders.

   A three-step scheme will help the editor to keep these three
speeds clearly separated, yet interrelated properly to yield the
copy he wants.

   1. Determine what the *tape speeds* are, i.e., what the play-
       ing speed of the master is, and what playing speed is
       desired for the copy.

   2. Determine the *dubbing speeds*. For every speed setting on
       the feed machine above or below the playing speed of the
       master, set the receive machine an equal number of set-
       tings in the same direction from the desired playing
       speed of the copy.

   3. Check the *recorder speeds* to see whether the dubbing
       speed settings are possible. If they are not, it will be
       necessary to figure out an alternate pair of dubbing
       speeds.

   A summary of steps one and two above is provided in Appendix 6. However, problems may arise with step three if one of
the ideal speeds recommended by the first two steps is not
available on the recorders being used. Dubbing, then, cannot be
carried out in one operation. The editor must stairstep the
speeds by going through the dubbing process more than once in
order to achieve the desired playing speed for the copy. The
first dubbing operation alters the speed of the copy in the direction of the desired speed. Subsequent dubbing, using the
copy on the feed machine as the *new master*, will complete the
change. Because of the loss of quality, stairstepping should be
avoided if at all possible.

   The following TIP captures the major points about dubbing
made in this discussion:

TIP: To make a dub of the highest possible quality from an original recording, use two machines with identical or closely matched impedances. Clean and demagnetize the heads of both machines. Then, at the fastest speed possible, feed the original recording from the machine on which it was made to the receive machine. If practical, avoid making a copy with a playing speed slower than the playing speed of the original.

A simple guide to dubbing procedures is contained in the following sequence of steps. Read across the page from feed recorder to receive recorder.

Feed Recorder	Receive Recorder
Line from *output* jack.	Line to *input* jack.
Set speed at fastest possible.	Set speed at fastest possible.
Put on original recording.	Put on blank tape.
Adjust output volume to natural loudness.	Switch to AVC if desired, or if using manual control, adjust volume by the trial-run procedure.
Place in playback mode *after* beginning to record at the receive machine.	Place in record mode *before* beginning to play at the feed machine.

The trial-run procedure mentioned in this guide is outlined in Chapter 6 in the section on volume control.

An evaluation of the dubbing technique is offered in the following TIPS:

PROS: (1) Dubbing can be used for the full range of editing operations: removing, adding, rearranging. (2) It is equally useful for open-reel and cassette tape. (3) It can be used for tape with any number of tracks. (4) The tone, volume, track, speed, or format (cassette or open-reel) of the original recording can be modified on the copy as desired. (5) Fade-in and fade-out effects can be obtained by manipulating the input or the output volume control. (6) Dubbing can be done quickly using speeds faster than the playing speed of the master.[2] (7) No gaps in the copy need occur when original material is omitted. (8) Record mode clicks can be avoided on open-reel copies. (9) The tape backing is not weakened.

CONS: (1) Two recorders with closely matched impedances are required for dubbing. (2) There is an inevitable loss of

quality in the transfer. (3) Because of the time lag necessary for the feed machine to reach normal speed, dubbing is
not useful for close and ultraclose editing. (4) Nor is it
useful for short sections (several seconds long). (5) Record mode clicks cannot be avoided when the machine is a
cassette.

The characteristics of all the editing techniques discussed
in this chapter are summarized in Figure 15.

COMBINING EDITING TECHNIQUES

The editor should not think that he must weigh the pros and
cons and select one and only one editing technique for his job.
While each technique has certain inherent disadvantages, the
editor will find that by combining techniques, he can sometimes
avoid every one of the disadvantages. At other times, his combination of techniques simply trades off a more serious problem
for a less serious one. Nevertheless, the trade-off will often
result in a superior editing job. Some of the more common
multitechnique situations are mentioned.

Open-Reel Editing Problems

Since splicing and pen erasing affect all tracks on a tape,
the editor faces a problem when he wants to use these techniques
on only one of adjacent tracks of recording. To apply these
techniques to his material, but also preserve the nearby tracks,
the editor must first dub to another tape the track he wishes to
edit. Editing may then proceed.

Another problem is that dubbing and machine-fed head erasing
are not suited to begin at close and ultraclose boundaries.
Neither technique, however, is precluded for close and ultraclose editing. In the case of dubbing, if the original material
is cut at its beginning and leader tape is added to it, the dubbing may be done as usual. As for erasing a long section of material which begins at a *tight* point, head erasing should be
done by hand at the beginning and then finished by the recorder.

At times the editor may have a problem figuring out how to
get the right amount of silence after removing material. Head
or pen erasing will leave a gap; splicing leaves none. If a
full gap is too much silence, and none is too little, the editor
may want to erase first, then splice out just enough of the gap
to leave the desired length of silence.

Editing by splicing, of course, weakens the tape backing. A
weakened tape and joints which may eventually come apart are
drawbacks to splicing, unless the signal on the spliced tape is
dubbed to a splice-free tape for preservation.

Pur-pose	Method	Ma-chine*	Affects Nearby Tracks	Editing Close	Editing Ultra close	Sections† Short	Sections† Long	Damages Tape	Preserves Original Quality	Leaves Gap	Leaves Noise	For Fading Effects
	Characteristics											
To Remove	ERASE HEAD											
	Machine-fed	O	−	−	−	−	+	−	−	+	−	−
		C	−	−	−	−	+	−	−	+	+	−
	Hand-fed	O	−	+	+	+	−	−	−	+	−	−
		C	+	+	+	+	−	−	−	+	−	−
	EDIT PEN											
	Machine-fed	O	+	−	−	−	+	−	−	+	+	+
	Hand-fed	O/C	+	+	−	+	−	−	−	+	+	+
To Remove, Add or Rearrange	SPLICING	O/C	+	+	+	+	+	+	+	−	−	−
	DUBBING	O	−	−	−	−	+	−	−	−	−	+
		C	−	−	−	−	+	−	−	−	+	+

*O = Open reel; C = Cassette   †Short = a few seconds

Fig. 15. Summary of Editing Techniques

Cassette Editing Problems

While there are numerous problems facing the editor who
wants to perfect his cassette recordings, the major problems
arise from the slow recording speed and enclosed tape which
make it difficult to do close and ultraclose editing, and the
construction of the cassette recorder which prevents easy access
to the heads.

Although it is potentially possible to handle every cassette
editing problem by treating the tape like open-reel tape, the
editor who prefers simpler procedures is not left without re-
course. The simplest solution for a number of problems--access
for splicing, slow speeds, multitrack tape--is to dub the tape
track to be edited to an open-reel tape, increasing the speed
to 3 3/4 ips or 7 1/2 ips. This will spread out the signal on
one track for accurate splicing, head erasing, and so on. After
editing, the material can be transferred back to the cassette
format. Because this last transfer is from a dub and must be
done at normal playing speed, since the cassette machine has
only one speed, quality loss will be somewhat greater than
normal.

When head erasing or dubbing on a cassette recorder, record
mode clicks are inevitable. The edit pen can be used efficiently
to remove these clicks.

The ability to edit relieves the recordist of much worry when
recording in less-than-ideal circumstances. If the recordist is
a skillful editor, he can tolerate a great deal more noise than
he could were it impossible to edit his recordings. Ultimately,
the only intolerable noise is the one simultaneously recorded
with the signal.

Appendixes

Power Supply for Using Recording Equipment Abroad

The local power situation should determine (1) the power requirement of the recorder you take into a particular area, and/or (2) the auxiliary equipment that may be necessary to supply power to your recorder.

In Chapter 1, we discussed the power requirement of recorders and the circumstances for which each power category is most applicable. In this appendix, we are interested primarily in the auxiliary equipment necessary to accommodate the particular requirements of recorders. Equipment may be for either AC-only or for AC/DC recorders.

The simplest solution to an irregular or nonexistent local power supply is to use an AC/DC recorder on batteries only. A discussion of batteries is presented below. If you have an AC-only recorder or an AC/DC recorder which you want to use on AC supply for running the recorder or for recharging batteries, there is another, although not entirely satisfactory, way around irregular or nonexistent electrical power, namely, by using a small AC generator.

Gasoline powered generators (weighing from thirty-five to sixty-five pounds) are available. They can reliably and inexpensively deliver regulated AC power no matter where you may be. However, by most comparisons--initial cost, quietness, convenience--the generator is a poor second to batteries for an AC/DC machine or to the equipment needed to run an AC machine using an irregular power supply. The alternatives are spelled out below.

AC-Only Recorders

For AC-only recorders, two different situations may be considered: (1) foreign AC supply, and (2) foreign DC supply.

Depending on where you are in the world, AC supply may vary
widely. If you are in Africa, the voltage may range from 110-
250 volts with any one of ten to fifteen different voltage
points in that range according to your location. The same is
true for Asia, Europe, and Oceania.

The first consideration is how to transform the available AC
supply into 110-120 volts to power the recorder. If the supply
is within that range, no extra equipment will be necessary. But
if the supply is greater than 110-120 volts, a *step-down transformer* will be needed.

The second consideration is how to control fluctuating voltage. In some areas, the voltage fluctuates, for example, from
90 volts to 135 volts for a nominal 115-volt current. A *voltage
regulator* will be needed to supply the recorder with steady current. If the fluctuation is too extreme, the safety of the recorder will be in danger.

A third consideration is the frequency of the AC supply. If
the recorder accepts only 60-cycle current, and the available
supply is anywhere from 25-76 cycles, some *cycle adjustment* will
be necessary. For example, if the current has the common 50-
cycle frequency, and your recorder is designed for 60 cycles, a
change in the machine is necessary so that the tape speeds
(7 1/2, 3 3/4 ips, etc.) will remain constant, and so that tapes
made on 50- or 60-cycle recorders can be used interchangeably.
Without an adjustment, tapes recorded with 60-cycle current will
sound slow on 50 cycles; those recorded with 50-cycle current
will sound fast on 60 cycles.

All cycle adjustments require some change in the recorder itself. Short of purchasing a new recorder, there are three common methods used to provide the needed change to operate on different cycle power. If the different power supply will not
damage the motor, the easiest change is a replacement of the
capstan, substituting one with a circumference which will compensate for the cycle difference. The second method used is a
gear change which may be installed by a recorder serviceman or
may be built into the machine by the manufacturer and activated
by a switch. A third change is brought about by replacing the
AC motor with one designed for the power supply of the particular frequency. Different manufacturers use different methods
for handling the problem of cycle differences. Standard cycle
adjustments are commonly available for changes between 50- and
60-cycle operation.

If the supply available is DC, whether 6, 12, 28, 32 volts or 110 to 440 volts (as in Europe), then an *inverter* is needed to change the DC into regulated 110-120 volts AC with 60-cycle frequency. Some small units are designed to be mounted under the dash of a car or truck and plugged into the cigarette lighter socket.

AC/DC Recorders

For AC/DC recorders, no extra equipment is needed if batteries are available. If new batteries are not continuously available, then regulated AC will be needed to power the recorder or to recharge a rechargeable battery system. In cases where the available AC or DC supply is not appropriate for the needs of the recorder, conversion equipment of the kind described above will be necessary, except that no auxiliary equipment is necessary for cycle differences.

There are various options open to the recordist for battery power. In our estimation, the most viable options are the carbon-zinc cell, the alkaline cell, and the nickel-cadmium (ni-cad) cell.

TIP: The rechargeable battery is technology's gift to the tape recordist. However, if no power is available to charge the battery, the expendable carbon-zinc cell is the best choice when batteries must be purchased abroad. The long life nonrechargeable alkaline cell will be the best battery to take abroad.

The rechargeable alkaline cell is an inexpensive way to have all the advantages of rechargeability. A ni-cad system involves a considerable investment, but it is a once-in-a-lifetime purchase. The choice of one system over the other may rest on how extensively battery power is needed (if extensive, choose ni-cad), the availability of continuous recharging power (if not continuous, choose alkaline), the risk of leakage (if low risk is wanted, choose ni-cad), and economy (if important, choose alkaline).

Determining Recording Time for Open-Reel Tape

In the chart below, the relationships among reel size, backing thickness, tape length, recorder speeds, and time for metric and nonmetric systems are captured.

Certain of these categories require some comment. First, two 1/2-mil backings are listed for 5- and 7-inch reels. The second has a thinner oxide coating than the first, which enables the manufacturer to wind more tape on a reel.

Second, in the categories of tape length and recorder speeds, the conventional metric and nonmetric figures are not conversion equivalents. All metric lengths are shorter than the corresponding foot lengths. For example, 45 meters is more than two feet less than 150 feet; 1460 meters is about 10 feet less than 4800 feet. All the metric speeds are slower than their corresponding inch speeds. Since 19 centimeters is more than an inch less than 7 1/2 inches, the tape on a metric recorder must travel slower in one second of time than on a nonmetric recorder.

Third, these facts about tape length and recorder speed converge in the time category. The slower cm/s speeds use up the shorter length of tape in almost precisely the same amount of time as the faster ips speeds use up the longer length of tape. The difference in each case is only a matter of seconds. For this reason, the two sets of recording times can be collapsed to one chart.

The time figures given here are not those typically listed on a box of tape. Manufacturers very generally cite record/playback time by the quarter, half, or full hour. While easier to remember, it is only roughly correct; the time actually available is somewhat more than is cited. The cumulative effect of the error is considerable. The by-the-hour calculation says that 4800 feet of tape played at 15/16 ips will last 16 hours (because 2400 feet lasts 8 hours, 1200 feet lasts 4 hours, 600 feet lasts 2 hours, and 300 feet lasts 1 hour). The fact is, however, that 4800 feet will last slightly over 17 hours.

To figure recording time accurately, the following formulas have been devised for metric and nonmetric recordings.

$$\text{Recording Time (in minutes)} = \frac{\text{Tape Length (in feet)}}{\text{Tape Speed (ips) x 5}}$$

$$\text{Recording Time (in minutes)} = \frac{\text{Tape Length (in meters)}}{\text{Tape Speed (cm/s) x .6}}$$

The times given in the chart are for *recording in one direction*. To determine the total time on a two-track monophonic or a four-track stereophonic recording, multiply the time by two. The total time on a four-track monophonic recording is the time given multiplied by four.

	Tape Length		Recorder Speeds			
	Feet	Meters	15/16 ips 2.375 cm/s	1 7/8 ips 4.75 cm/s	3 3/4 ips 9.5 cm/s	7 1/2 ips 19 cm/s
3" reel — 1½ mil	150'	45m	0:32	0:16	0:08	0:04
1 mil	225'	68m	0:48	0:24	0:12	0:06
½ mil	300'	90m	1:04	0:32	0:16	0:08
¼ mil	600'	180m	2:08	1:04	0:32	0:16
5" reel — 1½ mil · 1 mil ·	900'	270m	3:12	1:36	0:48	0:24
½ mil ·	1200'	360m	4:16	2:08	1:04	0:32
½ mil ·	1800'	540m	6:24	3:12	1:36	0:48
¼ mil ·	2400'	730m	8:32	4:16	2:08	1:04
7" reel — 1½ mil · 1 mil · ½ mil ·	3600'	1100m	12:48	6:24	3:12	1:36
½ mil · ¼ mil ·	4800'	1460m	17:04	8:32	4:16	2:08

Recording Time of One Pass Using Open-Reel Tape

Tape Tests

The following tape tests should be helpful in making on-the-spot checks on the quality of open-reel recording tape. A good tape will pass all of these tests.

Backing Characteristics

1. Test to Determine Backing Material

    See page 82 for the *light test* and *tear test* used to distinguish acetate, polyester, and PVC backings.

2. Test for Proper Tape Winding

    Good Tape: Each layer of the new tape is wound smoothly on top of the last layer.

    Poor Tape: Layers of the new tape may be loose or uneven. This indicates improper tension on the tape. Improper tension may make the tape width greater than 1/4 inch in some places, a defect which results in wow and flutter and poor tracking.

3. Test for Flexibility

    Extend a few inches of tape off the edge of a table or other flat surface. Compare the degree of bending with a tape of the same thickness which you know to be flexible.

    Good tape: Tape limply bends over the edge.

Poor Tape: Tape does not hang limply, but stands out almost
             straight from the table edge. Poor flexibility
             means poor tape-to-head contact with resultant
             loss of high frequencies and volume. Poor
             flexibility may result from dried out backing
             or dried out binder material.

Coating Characteristics

1. Test for Presence of Primer

    See page 86 for the test to determine whether or not primer
    was applied before the coating material.

2. Test for the Quality of Binder.

    Hold a pencil in your hand, sharpened end up. Fit the point
    into the spindle hole of a reel of tape so that the reel is
    parallel to the floor. Let several inches of tape begin to
    unwind and fall off the reel.

    Good Tape: Tape layers will continue to unwind.

    Poor Tape: Tape does not unwind freely, one layer sticking
                to the next. The gumminess causing the sticking
                will increase wow and flutter. If bits of coat-
                ing are pulled off when the layers are separated
                from each other, any signal will be lost at that
                point. Gumminess may derive from poor binder
                compound being affected by temperature and
                winding pressures.

3. Tests for Smooth and Evenly Applied Oxide Coating

    a. Check for Smoothness of Coating

        Gently rub a few inches of the coated side of the tape
        over your lower lip. A little practice comparing oxide
        smoothness is helpful.

        Good Tape: Tape will feel very smooth. A lubricated
                    tape will feel almost slick.

        Poor Tape: Tape will feel rough. The roughness works
                    like sandpaper on the recorder heads.

    b. Check for Evenly Applied Coating

        Hold a short piece of tape in front of a strong light.
        Good Tape: Tape will show no irregularities.

      Poor Tape: Tape may show holes (uncoated spots on the tape), dark nodules where clumps of oxide particles (agglomerates) are, or streaks of light and dark coating. The result of poor coating is poor recording.

4. Tests for Loose Oxide Particles

    a. Apply a piece of cellophane tape to the coated surface of the tape. Then, quickly pull it off.

        Good Tape: No loose oxide should adhere to the cellophane tape.

        Poor Tape: Oxide flakes will adhere to the cellophane tape.

    b. Clean the recorder heads thoroughly. Then run the tape in the playback mode for a few minutes. With a fresh cotton swab, clean the heads again.

        Good Tape: No oxide residue will be present on the cotton.

        Poor Tape: Oxide particles will show up on the cotton swab. Loose particles gum up the recorder heads, capstan, and tape guides. This can cause speed inaccuracies as well as loss of good sound reproduction.

White-Box Tape

The three main types of *white-box* or off-brand open-reel tape are listed and evaluated below.

1. Standard Audio Tape

   a. Used Tape. Used polyester tape from radio stations and recording studios is probably one of the best buys in inexpensive tape. But avoid acetate tape because it tends to break easily after several years.

   b. Outside Cuts. Tape is manufactured in wide rolls, then slit to one-quarter-inch widths. The two or four outside slits from the wide rolls of tape often contain agglomerates or uneven coating and are definitely inferior. These outside cuts may be made by manufacturers of name-brand tape but sold under a different name. Of course, the manufacturer makes no claim of quality nor does he make any guarantee on the tape.

   c. Spliced Ends. These may be a bargain if all the pieces of tape on a reel are the same kind of tape. If the local tape dealer has done the splicing himself, chances are that the tape is a mixture of various kinds of tape, making it a high risk.

2. Rejected Computer Tape Reslit to One-Quarter Inch

   Oftentimes, the reslitting causes variations in tape width which will result in partial loss of volume. This tape,

usually black in color, was not originally designed for
audio use and will not produce high quality recordings.

3. Cheaply Made Tape

Cheap tape made cheaply by skimping all the way around is no
bargain because of the damage it can do to your recorder.
The oxide usually flakes off, causing the binder to stick
to recorder heads like chewing gum. The slitting is often
uneven. There is no primer, not even the brushing off of
loose particles. This tape often sells for little more
than the price of a good reel.

Increasing or Decreasing Silent Spaces in a Recording by Splicing

The following simple scheme may be used to determine how much blank tape or leader tape should be added to or removed from a tape recording in order to yield the length of silence desired.

1. How many seconds of silence do you want in all?   _____

2. How many seconds of silence are now present?   _____

3. How many seconds must be added to the tape?

                                         Subtract 2 from 1   _____

   Or, how many seconds must be subtracted?

                                          Subtract 1 from 2   _____

4. At what speed is the recording made?   _____

5. How many inches of tape must be added or subtracted?

                                         Multiply 3 by 4   _____

Determining
Dubbing Speeds

The amount of increase in tape recorder noise and wow and flutter from the master to the copy can be minimized by dubbing at the fastest possible speed. The chart below identifies which speeds should be used for fastest dubbing.

To use the chart, find the playing speed of the master tape in the far left column. On the same line, opposite this speed in the far right column, find the speed you want as the playing speed of the copy. Set your feed and receive machines at the speeds indicated on that same line in the center two columns. For example, let us say that the master tape was recorded at 3 3/4 ips, and that we want a copy to play at 1 7/8 ips. The chart indicates that we should set the feed machine at 7 1/2 ips and the receive machine at 3 3/4 ips in order to make the copy at the fastest possible dubbing speed.

Fastest Dubbing Speed

Speed of Master	Set Feed Machine at	Set Receive Machine at	Speed of Copy
	↓	↓	
7 1/2 ips	7 1/2 ips	7 1/2 ips	7 1/2 ips
7 1/2	7 1/2	3 3/4	3 3/4
7 1/2	7 1/2	1 7/8	1 7/8
7 1/2	7 1/2	15/16	15/16
3 3/4 ips	3 3/4 ips	7 1/2 ips	7 1/2 ips
3 3/4	7 1/2	7 1/2	3 3/4
3 3/4	7 1/2	3 3/4	1 7/8
3 3/4	7 1/2	1 7/8	15/16
1 7/8 ips	1 7/8 ips	7 1/2 ips	7 1/2 ips
1 7/8	3 3/4	7 1/2	3 3/4
1 7/8	7 1/2	7 1/2	1 7/8
1 7/8	7 1/2	3 3/4	15/16
15/16 ips	15/16 ips	7 1/2 ips	7 1/2 ips
15/16	1 7/8	7 1/2	3 3/4
15/16	3 3/4	7 1/2	1 7/8
15/16	7 1/2	7 1/2	15/16

Overseas Recording Outfit

The following is a checklist of equipment and supplies you may want to have on hand in order to be properly prepared to record wherever you are.

Basic Recording Equipment

    Recorder to meet your needs

        Socket adapter--purchase abroad

        Voltage conversion device, if needed

        Cycle conversion device--purchase from dealer

        Voltage regulator, if needed

    Patch cords

    Microphone suited to your needs

    Supply of recording tape suited to your situation

    Battery tester (for DC cells, if they are purchased abroad)

Supplies for Recorder Care

    Head demagnetizer (AC or DC)

    Head cleaning fluid

    Cotton swabs

Toothpicks for cleaning pressure pads

Extra pressure pads (with adhesive backing)

Strobe for checking speed accuracy (optional)

Tone tape for head azimuth alignment (optional)

Recorder cover or case

Airtight bag, dehumidifying agent and indicator card (for
high humidity areas, if recorder is not tropicalized)

Supplies for Recorder Repair

Service manual and parts inventory for your recorder

Spare parts
   Drive belts (if recorder uses them)
   Rubber roller
   Other rubber parts

Tools
   Set of small screwdrivers
   Needle-nose pliers
   Hex key wrenches
   Soldering iron and solder

Lubricants
   Light lubricating oil (no thicker than SAE 10 with deter-
   gent additives)
   Silicone grease for sliding metal parts

Supplies for Tape Use and Care

Splicing tools and tape

Leader tape

Tape clips or spongies

Empty reels

Labels for identifying boxes

Editing pen

Notes

Chapter 1

1. The fact that a battery can light a bulb does not indicate the strength of the charge. The proper battery tester
should be of the type which will put the cell under some load in
order to get a true charge rating.

2. If a steady 3000 Hz tone recorded on tape fluctuates when
played back by a maximum or an average of ±3 Hz (2997-3003 Hz)
instead of remaining steady, the wow and flutter is by definition
0.1 percent or one part distortion in a thousand. The frequency
with which the fluctuation occurs in one second defines wow as
opposed to flutter. If the fluctuation occurs 1 to 10 times per
second, it is wow; if it is 10 to 300 times per second, it is
flutter.

There are two principal ways to measure wow and flutter, each
yielding different figures. One calculation gives peak (*maximum*
wobble in the example above) wow and flutter; the other method
produces root mean square, rms (*average* wobble in the example
above), wow and flutter. There is no consistent mathematical
relationship between the two. The rms values, however, are always smaller than peak values and are generally the values cited
in specifications. The recommendations in the TIP are in rms
values.

3. Some home recorders have as many as six heads. Some
automatically reversing machines have a duplicate set of erase,
record, and playback heads. Each additional head, while expensive in itself, may add a significant amount of costly electronics to the recorder.

4. Decibel was named in honor of Alexander Graham Bell. It is generally accepted that one or two decibels is the smallest change in the strength of a steady tone detectable by the human ear.

5. If the frequency response varies no more than ±3 db across the range of 50 Hz-15,000 Hz, it is considered essentially a *flat* response.

6. There are two major conditions that should be mentioned. First, the tape used on the recorder must be compatible with the *bias* setting of the recorder. Bias is the ultrahigh frequency current fed into the record head along with the signal which enables the head to magnetize the tape oxide in proportion to the magnetism emitted by the record gap. We can approach ideal recorder-tape compatibility by following the recommendations in Chapter 4.

Second, an optimized recorder uses *standard equalization*. A brief explanation of equalization follows. Because of the size of some magnetic particles on the tape in relation to the width of the head gap, some frequencies are stronger or weaker than they should be. Equalization, as the name implies, decreases the intensity of some frequencies and boosts the intensity of other frequencies during record (pre-equalization) and playback (post-equalization). The result is that all frequencies in the range maintain their proper balance.

Equalization is necessary for every tape recorder, but not all recorder manufacturers use standard equalization. If a recorder has standard equalization, a note will appear on the specification sheet which may read: record/playback equalization: NAB, MIRA, or DIN (for European machines). If the standard is not used, the tape recorder will not be able to play successfully tapes made on other recorders and cannot make tapes to be played successfully on other recorders. Prerecorded tapes should have the same equalization as the recorders they are played on.

7. A frequency response of at least 50 Hz-15,000 Hz is considered essential for high fidelity sound reproduction. Generally, FM broadcasts do not have any program material outside the 30 Hz-15,000 Hz range.

8. Unfortunately, different manufacturers use different reference points in their procedures to arrive at the S/N ratio. Within the industry, the standard reference point is a harmonic distortion level of 3 decibels. The S/N figures can be weighted (to approximate our perception of sound) or unweighted. Weighted figures will be 5-7 decibels higher than the unweighted figures.

The ratios listed in the TIP are weighted and referenced to the 3-decibel level of distortion. However, S/N figures can be exaggerated enormously by recording at higher levels and letting the distortion level rise to 5-10 decibels. Since the industry standard is not being used universally, the harmonic distortion level must be known (even when the calculation is referenced to 0-VU) in order to interpret S/N specifications and compare them from recorder to recorder. Without this information, S/N ratios are not very informative. For this reason, you should not let the S/N figures be the deciding factor in selecting a particular recorder unless other test information is provided.

9. Monophonic recorders are popularly, though less correctly, called monaural recorders. Monaural is an older term, meaning literally *one ear*.

Stereophonic should not be confused or used synonymously with binaural, *two ears*. While stereo recording may use only two tracks simultaneously, it may use more than two. Binaural recording uses only two tracks, one for each of the two microphones placed close together in order to duplicate the relative position and pickup characteristics of the human ears. Binaural playback is through binaural headphones. Stereo recording may use two or more microphones, widely placed, and playback is generally through similarly placed speakers.

Since quadraphonic machines will not be treated in detail, a helpful discussion of this format can be found in William Cawlfield, "Four Channel Sound: What, How and When."

10. The presence of an unerased guard band is of no concern if the tape continues to be used on a four-track machine. The guard band becomes a problem only when the tape is played on a two-track machine in order to listen to something recorded by the four-track recorder. The two-track head will pick up the four-track material, but it will also pick up simultaneously the unerased material in the guard band.

11. A remote pause control usable at any distance from the recorder can be made quite easily for a recorder which has a *remote* jack. Many recorders have two jacks at the mike input. The larger hole is a mini jack for the microphone signal; the other, a submini jack, is for the remote on-off switch housed in the microphone. This jack is really a circuit breaker. To use it, locate an inexpensive earphone like those used with transistor radios with a submini plug on one end and an earphone on the other. Cut off the earphone, exposing the copper wire ends. When you plug into the submini jack and touch the wire ends together, you will find the recorder will operate whether it is in play or record. Separate the wires, breaking the

circuit, and the recorder stops. Connect the bare wire ends to
a simple switch, pushbutton or otherwise, available at any hardware store, and this completes the pause control.

12. The counter and tape timer are not the only methods for
quickly locating recording sections. Other visual methods are
also used, such as leader tape insertions, index tabs, and calibrated scales on tape reels or magazines. A variety of sensing
devices are also used for automatic place-finding within a reel
(cueing). Of the visual methods, leader tape and tabs are the
most accurate, then counter readings on the same recorder, and
least accurate is the scale.

Chapter 2

1. If it is not possible to have your recorder tropicalized,
you may want to do it yourself. All the necessary compounds can
be found in a paint or floor-covering store. First, all the
electrical components of the recorder should be cleaned with
chlorothane (not trichlorothane or acetone which may attack some
components) or hexachloraphene. Chlorothane can be found in
spray cans and will dry in a few minutes. Second, paint all
surfaces (except tuner, tube sockets) with polyurethane (preferably PC-18). Polyurethane is used in place of varnish on
some floor coverings. (Courtesy of Chemistry Lab, Magnavox
Company, Urbana, Illinois.)

2. Leonard P. Kubiak, "Tape Recorder Maintenance Program,"
p. 68.

Chapter 3

1. One of the authors built a shotgun microphone on the
model provided in J. R. Hollinger and J. E. Mulligan, "Build the
Shotgun Sound Snooper." Nineteen instead of 37 tubes were used;
the maximum length was 23 3/4 inches with tube lengths differing
by an interval of 1/4 inch. Thin-wall tubing of the correct
outside diameter is available from a number of sources. Tubing
is least expensive when purchased from a steel distributing firm
in twelve-foot lengths; it is most expensive in aluminum arrow
shafts (28 to 29 inches long). A three-watt battery-operated
amplifier was purchased prefabricated from Lafayette Radio
Electronics.

2. Arthur E. Robertson, *Microphones*, p. 349. See Chapter 1,
the section entitled Record/Playback System, for an explanation
and discussion of frequency response and smoothness (decibel
variation).

3. Peter B. Denes and Elliot N. Pinson, *The Speech Chain*, p. 150. Some high schools and universities make foreign language material available to students by means of an automatic tele-phone-answering hookup. A student may dial the appropriate number from anywhere at any time, and the tape will be played auto-matically over the telephone. One caution should be mentioned about this technique. Since the telephone frequency range is so limited, there is often not an adequate amount of information in the transmission for nonnative speakers of a language to dis-criminate fine phonetic differences. Thus, while the telephone technique is useful for some phases of language study, it should be employed only in a limited way for pronunciation drills.

4. Robertson, *Microphones*, p. 350.

5. *Ibid.*, p. 279.

6. Full specifications and assembling instructions for a parabolic dish reflecting microphone may be found in Rakes, *Solid State Electronic Projects*, pp. 109-115.

Chapter 4

1. One of the inherent problems in recording is that the mag-netic properties of recording tape do not permit the tape par-ticles to be magnetized in proportion to the magnetism of the signal at the head. Consequently, the recorded signal will sound grossly distorted on playback. This fault is remedied by mixing a very high frequency signal (called an AC bias current) with the recorded signal during recording functions. This super-sonic signal, usually five times the highest frequency the head can record, minimizes the distortion so that the recorded signal will sound true when played back. For best results, the bias current must be set for the magnetic characteristics of a par-ticular kind of tape.

2. Jan Rahm, "The Right Tape for the Job," p. 53.

3. Tape recorder manufacturers who also make recording tape will often use their own standard tape as the basis for bias and equalization settings, and they will suggest that a recorder owner use their tape. Other recorder makers may use Scotch 111, the widely recognized standard of the industry, as the basis for their settings.

4. Part of print-through reduction is achieved by giving re-cordings proper care. For a discussion of measures especially helpful in print-through reduction, see Chapter 5 in the section on protecting the signal.

5. A partial list of current name-brand tapes on the market
in the United States is the following: Advent, Ampex, Audiotape,
BASF, Capitol, Certron, DAK, Irish (Ampex), Maxell, Memorex,
Norelco, Primus, RCA, Scotch (3M), Sony, Soundcraft (Reeves),
TDK, Tracs, Wabash.

6. See note five for a list of name-brand tape manufacturers.

Chapter 6

1. Since no microphone is used, external noise is an irrelevant factor for direct-line recording.

2. A simple windscreen can be made from a folded cloth
attached with a rubber band to the mike so that the cloth forms
a wall around the mike face. For a discussion of windscreens,
see Chapter 3 in the section on microphone accessories.

3. William J. Samarin, *Field Linguistics*, p. 96.

4. A brief but helpful discussion of music recording techniques is given in George W. Cushman, "Recording Musical Instruments," pp. 40, 44, 46.

Chapter 7

1. It is this type of control that is necessary in the production of language laboratory masters. For drill construction,
see references to Lado, Larson and Smalley, Stack. For language
laboratory design and use, see references to Stack and especially
the *National Association of Language Laboratory Directors
Journal.*

2. In our own research, it is our personal preference to use
overt techniques whenever we record adult speech; however, we do
not feel this is necessary when recording young children. In
preparing the material of this chapter, we have tried to avoid
prejudging the propriety of covert recording for other recordists
and have presented a variety of overt and covert techniques. In
all cases, the covert techniques may be used overtly, that is,
with the knowing consent of subjects, although the equipment may
remain out of sight. For a helpful discussion of fieldwork
ethics, see Wolfram and Fasold, *The Study of Social Dialects in
American English,* pp. 46-48.

3. Radio and electronics suppliers sell these microphones in
easy-to-assemble kits for a few dollars or preassembled for

somewhat more. Even though the mikes are small--a few are the size of a pack of cigarettes--some mikes come equipped with volume controls and jacks into which some other sound source (radio, TV, tape recorder) can be plugged for broadcasting. The operator of an FM mike is not required to have a license.

4. For other purposes, the combination of FM mike and FM radio can be used as an inexpensive public address system. The speaker simply talks into the mike and lets the radio amplifier boost his voice to the desired volume.

Chapter 8

1. The tape is not actually demagnetized by the edit pen, but remagnetized by the one pole--north or south--of the magnet. This is the source of the hiss. Demagnetizers such as the head demagnetizer, the erase head, or the bulk eraser leave the tape truly demagnetized--neither north nor south predominating in the oxide particles.

2. Since a speaker-to-mike connection between recorders is an alternative to a direct-line hookup, high-speed dubbing can be done over the telephone. Let us say that caller A has twenty minutes of information to convey to caller B in a long distance call. If caller A records the material at 15/16 ips, he can play the recording into the phone handset at 7 1/2 ips. If caller B is ready at the other end of the line with his tape recorder set at 7 1/2 ips, caller B can record the twenty minutes of material in less than three minutes. For the best reception, caller B should use a telephone pickup coil on the handset. After the call, he can play back the recording at the original 15/16 ips speed.

Bibliography

Angus, Robert. "75 Years of Magnetic Recording." *High Fidelity* 23 (March, 1973):42-50.

Brooks, Lee. "Service--Who Needs It?" *Tape Recording* 14 (January, 1967):32-35.

Cawlfield, William. "Four Channel Sound: What, How and When." *Popular Electronics Including Electronics World* 1 (June, 1972):26-31.

Crowhurst, Norman H. *ABC's of Tape Recording.* Indianapolis: Howard W. Sams and Co., 1961.

_____. "All About Tape Recorder Bias." *Radio-Electronics* 41 (March, 1970):40-42.

Cushman, George W. "Recording Musical Instruments." *Popular Photography* 52 (April, 1963):40, 44, 46.

Denes, Peter B., and Pinson, Elliot N. *The Speech Chain.* Bell Telephone Laboratories, 1963.

Dyar, T. Gerald. "Techniques and Devices: Microphone Placement." *Ethnomusicology* 5 (January, 1961):49-51.

_____. "Techniques and Devices: Microphones." *Ethnomusicology* 4 (September, 1960):137-141.

_____. "Techniques and Devices: Pitch Control." *Ethnomusicology* 4 (January, 1960):19-22.

Foster, Edward J. "How We Judge Tape Recorders." *High Fidelity* 17 (August, 1967):47-51.

Frank, M. "Like to Tape a School Band? Here Are Key Pointers." *Popular Photography* 71 (September, 1972):51-52.

Friedman, H. "There's Nothing Wrong with Tape Cartridges and Cassettes." *High Fidelity* 22 (March, 1972):48-57.

Grozny, I. L. "How to Choose a Tape Recorder." *High Fidelity* 18 (August, 1968):47-51.

Gudschinsky, Sara C. *How to Learn an Unwritten Language*. New York: Holt, Rinehart and Winston, 1967.

Hawk, James. "Tape-Recorder Wow and Flutter." *Electronics World* 81 (June, 1969):36-37, 58.

Hirsch, Julian D. "How to Select a Cassette Recorder." *Popular Electronics Including Electronics World* 2 (July, 1972):12-16.

_____. "Noise Reducing Systems for Cassettes." *Popular Electronics Including Electronics World* 4 (July, 1973):32-35.

_____. "A Seminar for Tape Recorder Buyers." *Stereo Review* 30 (March, 1973):60-66.

Hollinger, James R., and Mulligan, John E. "Build the Shotgun Sound Snooper." *Popular Electronics* 20 (June, 1964):51-54, 84.

Holt, J. "Cassettes for Perfectionists." *Popular Electronics Including Electronics World* 3 (March, 1973):12-16.

Kempler, Joseph. "How Recording Tape is Made." *Stereo Review* 30 (March, 1973):78-84.

Kubiak, Leonard P. "Cassette Tape Recorders—A New Breed." *Electronics World* 81 (June, 1969):24-36.

_____. "Selecting a Tape Recorder." *Electronics World* 81 (May, 1969):39, 62.

_____. "Tape Recorder Maintenance Program." *Electronics World* 80 (October, 1968):67-68.

Lado, Robert L. *Language Teaching: A Scientific Approach*. New York: McGraw-Hill, 1964.

Larson, Donald N., and Smalley, William A. *Becoming Bilingual*.
    New Canaan, Connecticut: Practical Anthropology, 1972.

Long, Jim. "A Microphone Primer: Basic Construction, Per-
    formance and Applications--Part II: Choosing and Applying."
    Audio 57 (January, 1973):34-44.

Mooney, Mark Jr. "The Magnetic Heads." *What You Should Know
    About Your Tape Recorder*. Flushing: Robins Industries Corp.,
    1963, pp. 40-45.

*The National Association of Language Laboratory Directors
    Journal* (Published at Ohio University, Athens, Ohio)

Nisbett, Alec. *The Technique of the Sound Studio*. 3rd Edition
    Revised. New York: Hastings House Publishers, 1973.

Rahm, Jan. "The Right Tape for the Job." *High Fidelity* 17
    (August, 1967):52-55.

Rakes, Charles D. *Solid State Electronic Projects*. Indianapolis:
    Howard W. Sams and Co., 1972.

Robertson, Arthur E. *Microphones*. 2nd Edition. New York:
    Hayden Book Co., 1963.

Salm, Walter. "Which Mikes for What Jobs." *Popular Mechanics*
    133 (June, 1970):92-95, 70f.

Samarin, William J. *Field Linguistics*. New York: Holt, Rine-
    hart and Winston, 1967.

Stack, Edward M. *The Language Laboratory and Modern Language
    Teaching*. Revised Edition. New York: Oxford University
    Press, 1966.

Tall, Joel and Clifford, Martin. *Your Tape Recorder*. New Hyde
    Park: Elpa Marketing Industries, 1965.

Tremaine, Howard M. *Audio Cyclopedia*. Indianapolis: Howard
    W. Sams and Co., 1969.

Vaughan, Denis. "Taping the Sounds of Quiet." *High Fidelity*
    22 (August, 1972):50-52.

Westcott, Charles G. "What You Can Do About Magnetic Head Wear."
    Tape Recording 16 (September-October, 1969):20-24.

_____, and Dubbe, Richard F. *Audels Practical
    Guide to Tape Recorders*. Indianapolis: Theodore Audels and
    Co., 1965.

Wokoun, William. "10 Steps to Best Mike Use." *Radio-Electronics* 41 (July, 1970):23-26, 79.

Wolfram, Walt, and Fasold, Ralph W. *The Study of Social Dialects in American English*. Englewood Cliffs, New Jersey: Prentice-Hall, 1974.

Zide, Larry. "Professional Hints for Amateur Tape Recordists." *High Fidelity* 19 (December, 1969):78-82.

_____. "Tape Up To Date." *High Fidelity* 21 (August, 1971):43-47.

Zuckerman, Arthur. *Getting the Most from Your Tape Recorder*. New Augusta, Indiana: Editors and Engineers, 1965.

Index

AC (alternating current): conversion equipment, 10, 166, 179; generator, 165. *See also* Tape recorder, power requirement of; Tape recorder, power supply for

Acetate tape backing, 81-82, 90, 171, 174; characteristics of, 82-83, 85; tests for, 82

Agglomerates, 87-88, 173, 174. *See also* Tape coating

Amplifier: auxiliary, 12, 132-33, 138-39, 184n.1; in microphone, 61, 71; in recorder, 7, 12, 22, 121

Automatic reverse. *See* Tape movement, automatic reverse

Automatic shutoff. *See* Tape movement, automatic shutoff

AVC (automatic volume control). *See* Recording volume, automatic control of

Azimuth. *See* Head, alignment of

Battery: charge, 16, 21, 127, 132, 138; condition indicator, 29; leakage, 50; power for recorder, 10-15; power from car, 11, 167; rechargeable, 11, 165, 167; supply, 126, 128; tester, 11, 179, 181n.1; types, 167

Bias, 89-92, 94, 182n.6, 185n.1, 185n.3

Bidirectional microphone, 59, 64-65, 72

Binaural recording, 183n.9

Binder. *See* Tape coating, binder

Bulk eraser, 40-41, 52, 54, 102-03, 128, 149, 187n.1. *See also* Magnet

Capstan, 89, 158; drive, 16-17; position of, in editing, 145-46, 150

Carbon pickup element, 68-69, 141

Cardioid microphone. *See* Unidirectional (cardioid) microphone

Cartridge machines, 6-9; tracks of, 8, 33

Cassette machines, 6, 8; automatic shutoff of, 21; battery indicator of, 29; characteristics of, 9, 18-19; covert recording with, 130-33, 137-38;